THE HOLY SPIRIT
Keys to the Kingdom

Gary Carroll

THE HOLY SPIRIT
Keys to the Kingdom

International Standard Book Number: 0-9673309-0-4

Heart

The smile on her face she shared with all.
A heart never dreaming of raising a wall.
But showing her love to even the small,
For loving each one was the depth of her call.

Something inside her that no one could see
Was a heart grown larger, a sheltering tree.
Covering others had caused it to grow,
A heart made ready for Him to show.

While the world was busy pursuing its dreams
Her heart stayed focused on heavenly things.
Her heart was grown for giving away
His love to a world clouded in grey.

Each day a difference that many would feel,
Her love causing hardness to instantly heal,
And a world began changing as one by one
Encountered a heart reflecting the Son.

Introduction

I am everywhere—both near and far,
in heaven and on earth. … Jeremiah 23:23–24 (CEV)

The American church is lacking in one necessary element for changing the world—knowing the person of God living here. The subject of personally meeting the Holy Spirit is generally never taught in church. So when the teaching does come forward, it immediately becomes suspect to many. It is a foreign teaching to many. It does not fit with traditional church sermons of the past. Tradition makes it almost impossible for many church members to desire a relationship with the Holy Spirit. For others, the believer must consider the new information and decide if it warrants an interest. It will take much time for many to endorse the message of personally meeting the Holy Spirit. It is time none of us have.

What is often found in church is a belief system. In many lives, this is Christianity—a system of beliefs that will eventually get them to heaven. And this is how God is usually comprehended, of living only in heaven.

A great deal of teaching is available concerning Jesus Christ. He is our Savior. He died on the cross for our sins and He made a way for us to be acceptable to His righteous Father. We owe Jesus everything. His teaching is vital. But meaningful teaching on the Holy Spirit is not so available. Sermons on personally meeting the Holy Spirit are almost unknown. The person of God living here is often forgotten.

There is a reason for this absence of teaching. Many of the teachers do not know the Holy Spirit personally so the subject is hardly addressed. This was never the intent of God. Jesus taught the disciples that they would know the Holy Spirit and that the Holy Spirit lived with them. This clear teaching is often lacking in a church.

Even when a reference is made to the Holy Spirit living here, the accompanying teaching that He is a person is rarely integrated. Many believe He is a force like the wind or the tongues of fire of Pentecost. And although He can reveal His presence in these ways, He is also a person, just as Jesus Christ and the Father are persons. There is an automatic disconnect in the minds of many believers to ever meeting the Holy Spirit. The fundamental teaching that He is a person is not realized.

One reason many shy away from the Holy Spirit is the King James mistranslation of His name. The name Holy Ghost does not accurately characterize who He is. Ghost implies an association with death, an inappropriate association for God. This mistranslated association is all our enemy needs to plant seeds of fear in the minds of the believer. Fear of the unknown has kept many from desiring to personally meet the Holy Spirit.

Others cannot see in scripture the need to pursue the Holy Spirit. These see our focus to be only on Jesus or only on the Father. But there is a clear teaching of Jesus where He instructed the disciples to ask for and seek the Holy Spirit. Many have not known His teaching.

Guilt can also prevent many from focusing on the Holy Spirit. These can feel they are betraying Jesus for any focus they entertain for the Holy Spirit. Yet the Bible teaches they are one God and that He is the Spirit of Jesus Christ.

All of these issues have prevented the church from presenting to the world the primary accomplishment of the cross. Jesus paid the ultimate price for every believer to live with God here. He made us acceptable so we could experience eternal life—knowing God, and it begins here, not in heaven. The fact that God the Holy Spirit lives here with us and is willing to step into our realm should be a primary focus of the church. He is the primary accomplishment of the cross. Unfortunately, He finds little focus. For many Christians He is overlooked, He is omitted and forgotten. The intent of this book is to reverse this antithesis.

Contents

Holy Spirit

You are welcome here

Chapter 1
THE HOLY SPIRIT

But he that is joined unto the Lord is one spirit.
1 Corinthians 6:17

Three days after the cross, Jesus was resurrected from the dead. After confirming His resurrection to many followers, He returned to heaven. There He provides our access to God the Father. All of our prayers to our Father will pass through Jesus. All of the answered prayers from our Father will pass through Jesus as well. Jesus is always in perfect union with the Father.

The Holy Spirit is here to include us in this union. Our union with the Holy Spirit provides our union with Jesus Christ. Our union with the Holy Spirit places us into the union of the Trinity. Everything accomplished on the cross is found in this all important union. Receiving what Jesus accomplished is also found in this union.

One Lord, one faith, one baptism,
One God and Father of all, who is above all,
and through all, and in you all. Ephesians 4:5–6

The Bible teaches us to recognize the three individuals of the Trinity. God the Father, God the Son and God the Holy Spirit are individual of each other, but are always in perfect union as one God. They are three in one. We see the three individuals of the Trinity throughout scripture. We should then realize that it is appropriate to address each member of the Godhead. So often, we omit the Holy Spirit from all that pertains to God. This is our first step to receiving from our Father. We must include Him. Jesus Christ and God the Father will not feel overlooked if much of our attention is directed to the Holy Spirit. They know how important He is in our Christian life. They have also witnessed the years of His omission in each of our lives.

...holy and reverend is his name. Psalm 111:9

The King James Version of the Bible translates the name Holy Spirit as the Holy Ghost. This unfortunate translation fails to characterize the Holy Spirit. The Holy Spirit is not a Ghost. He is Spirit. The word ghost embraces an image of death. The Holy Spirit is the God of the living, not the dead. He is the Spirit of life.

This translation also suggests that the Father and Jesus Christ must be Ghosts. The synonym is close, but certainly not accurate. The association of ghost will never harmonize with the person of God. The substance of God is Spirit.

We should always address the Holy Spirit by His proper name. His name is equally holy as the names of Jesus Christ and God the Father. God's names have always been very important to Him. Young's Literal Translation of the Holy Bible rightly translates His name as the Holy Spirit.

...but whatsoever he shall hear, that shall he speak:
and he will shew you things to come. John 16:13

The enemy has been able to blind many Christians to the fact of the Holy Spirit being a person. If we should believe this lie, we will never attempt a relationship with Him. If we cannot believe He is a person, we cannot believe much of the Bible. Scripture refers to Him as a person. Jesus referred to Him as a person. Many Christians have met Him as the person of God the Holy Spirit. Unfortunately, many Christians have trouble believing this. Much of tradition says He is not a person.

Many Christians see the power of the Holy Spirit as their objective. They imagine what they can do for God if they only had this power. Others see spiritual gifts as their benefit of the Holy Spirit. Still others see the fruits of the Spirit being their goal. All of these are wonderful because they are all of Him, but what about the person of the Holy Spirit? Do we forget the person who will give us these gifts? We should not be so focused on what we want to receive from Him. He is too wonderful and loving to be treated in this way. This type of relationship is like being the friend of a very wealthy man only because he gives us gifts. Our focus should be Him, the person, and not what we want to obtain from Him.

The Holy Spirit taught me years ago that if I seek the anointing I will receive nothing. If I will forget the anointing and seek Him, the person, He will anoint me. He is a person and I have known Him desiring to be reverenced and esteemed as God, the person of the Holy Spirit. When we meet Him as a person, our lives will no longer be satisfied with the world. We then realize how empty the activities of the world actually are. It becomes evident that there is no life outside of Him. When we meet Him, we understand He is the Spirit of life.

Jesus always referred to the Holy Spirit as a person. The personal pronouns *he* and *him* were used by Jesus as He referred to the Holy Spirit in John 16:13–15. Many verses of scripture refer to the Holy Spirit as a person by the use of personal pronouns. Unfortunate translations of Romans 8:16 and 8:26 refer to the Holy Spirit with the personal pronoun *itself*. The personal pronoun *himself* is found in Young's Literal Translation of the Holy Bible.

When we recognize the Holy Spirit as a person, just as Jesus Christ and God the Father are persons, we recognize that we can enter a relationship with Him. The relationship becomes exciting when we realize where He lives. He lives here! He not only lives in us, but He also lives with us.

> *But God hath revealed them unto us by his Spirit:*
> *for the Spirit searcheth all things,*
> *yea, the deep things of God. 1 Corinthians 2:10*

The Holy Spirit is a person and He has much deeper feelings than we have. His love is much deeper than ours and He can feel hurt much deeper than we can. He is holy. The holiness of His person continually risks being grieved by our sinful flesh. We can easily wound Him. This is why we often do not realize He is here with us. We force the Holy Spirit to shield Himself from our sinful nature. We should attempt to minimize our disobedient nature so that our relationship with the Holy Spirit will flourish. We will someday understand what a sacrifice the Holy Spirit makes to be with us here.

I have only known the Holy Spirit to be incredibly loving, giving and gentle. His expressed feelings are gentle because they are genuine. He also seems much more interested in giving to me rather than receiving from me. Many times, He has imparted His incredible power. His power is imparted powerfully at times and gently at other times. He is often overlooked because of His gentleness.

My first meeting with the Holy Spirit showed me how personal He is. I was finished praying as I began talking quietly to the Holy Spirit. I talked to Him as a person in the room with me. I asked if I could meet Him. I held out my hand to Him and asked Him to anoint me. He did. I began to feel the substance of God in the palm of my hand. It was a pleasant feeling. I was not afraid. I could also feel His love in the room with me. I learned that day how real our relationship could be.

The Holy Spirit will open our eyes to how God truly is. He is so different from the picture we often hold in our mind before we meet Him. His only nature is loving and never condemning. We also learn that He always desires us and that He will always pursue us.

> *And ye shall seek me, and find me, when ye shall*
> *search for me with all your heart. Jeremiah 29:13*

It is not as difficult as we might think to seek the Holy Spirit with all our heart. Desiring Him to this degree is a key to finding Him. God will always grant us the desires of our heart.

The loving, gentle nature of the Holy Spirit also requires the same nature in us to be expressed to Him. If we want Him to express His love to us, we should express our love for Him. Our relationship will be based on love.

One of the most important things we can do is invite the Holy Spirit to be with us. We should also welcome Him to be with us. Inviting and welcoming Him may seem basic, but it will do wonders in finding Him. He responds to an invitation and many times our invitation is needed. He interacts when He is desired, esteemed and welcomed.

Finding the Holy Spirit can be as easy as politely voicing that we want to be with Him. At other times, we may not immediately see a response. When we have trouble finding Him, we can ask Him to help us find Him. When we cannot seem to find Him, we can ask God the Father to ask the Holy Spirit to come to us. We can also express to Jesus that we want to be with His Spirit and ask Him to ask the Holy Spirit to visit us. The answer is always the same. The answer is yes. He gives us His best blessing in the Holy Spirit.

An important insight into finding the Holy Spirit is that to gain His presence, we often must lose our own presence. Prayer is the place we can apply this revelation. Even our thoughts can hinder us from drawing close to Him. He requires us to surrender to Him.

The Holy Spirit will also teach us to wait for Him. Much time in prayer may be spent waiting. He will reveal Himself to us when our flesh nature is out of His way and surrendered. We are dependent on Him, His timing and what He wants to do. The wait is always worth it. No matter how He reveals Himself to us, it will always be wondrous. Sometimes He will allow us to see His glory. Sometimes we will feel His tangible love. Sometimes He wants to touch us. Everything from Him is wonderful.

*If ye then, being evil, know how to give good gifts unto
your children: how much more shall your heavenly Father
give the Holy Spirit to them that ask him? Luke 11:13*

We should always place the Holy Spirit first on our prayer
list. We seek God with a true heart when we ask for Him
only and not what we want from Him. We ask for nothing,
yet we are asking for everything. The Holy Spirit holds
everything.

Once we meet the Holy Spirit personally, it becomes easy
to desire Him only. We will stop asking for things. Things
will mean so little. Things cannot compare with Him. He is
all we need. When we are close to the Holy Spirit, we
realize that He brings everything we need with Him. He
knows what we need before we ever ask. He teaches us to
trust Him to provide these needs. He teaches us to ask for
Him only.

*"And we are His witnesses to these things,
and so also is the Holy Spirit whom God has
given to those who obey Him." Acts 5:32 (NKJV)*

The promise of the Holy Spirit is found in our obedience.
This is quite an incentive. Our disobedience has the
opposite effect. It produces sin and guilt. These are
hindrances to staying close to Him. Our obedience removes
hindrances to our fellowship and will have the effect of
keeping us close to Him. Obedience develops from our
desire to stay close to Him.

...but ye know him; for he dwelleth with you, ... John 14:17

Developing a relationship with the Holy Spirit is a very important step forward for the Christian. So many Christians do not know Him. Lacking this relationship hinders the Holy Spirit from imparting the blessings of Jesus. A developed relationship allows this. It also liberates Him to help us keep these blessings. What a big job He has. He cannot be forgotten. His role in the Trinity is too important.

A relationship with the Holy Spirit begins with the recognition of Him dwelling with us. We often do not converse with Him because we do not see Him. We may think He is far away from us, but He is not. He is simply waiting for us to acknowledge Him. He has been pursuing us for years and we have mostly ignored Him. Now is our time to respond to Him. We can begin where we are. Acknowledge Him. He really is there. He is always present. Express to Him a desire to meet Him. Express love to Him. Worship Him as God the Holy Spirit. Offer your home to Him as a place where He is always welcome. Learn to consider the Holy Spirit as a family member and yet always esteem Him as an honored guest. If we mean what we are expressing, He will soon reveal that He is present. He wants this. He wants the relationship more than we do.

The Holy Spirit wants each Christian to meet Him in a personal way. He does not achieve this by pushing Himself on us. His nature is not to push. He is only willing to lead us into our relationship. A relationship reveals He is much closer than we think.

(baptizing them—to the name of the Father, and of the Son,
and of the Holy Spirit, …) Matthew 28:19
(Young's Literal Translation of the Holy Bible)

Occasionally, concerned Christians express that it is wrong to focus on the Holy Spirit. They say Jesus is to be our focus and not the Holy Spirit. This reasoning is not correct. Saying the Holy Spirit deserves less focus is saying He is less God. Jesus tells us why it is appropriate to focus on the Holy Spirit.

> *Verily, verily, I say unto you,* **He that receiveth whomsoever I send receiveth me**; *and he that receiveth me receiveth him that sent me. John 13:20*

> *Nevertheless I tell you the truth; It is expedient for you that I go away: for if I go not away, the Comforter will not come unto you; but if I depart,* **I will send him unto you**. *John 16:7*

Jesus told His disciples that someone would be sent to them to take His place with them. Would Jesus have said this to His disciples?

> "*I am sending you another person to take my place with you here, but I want you to neglect Him. You are not to spend much time with Him because I will be jealous of the time you spend with Him. It is expedient for you that I leave you because I will send Him to you, but remember, do not pay much attention to Him.*"

This sounds ridiculous, does it not? Many Christians believe this is the correct way to live the Christian life. I have attended churches where I was made to feel almost sinful for my focus on the Holy Spirit. The truth is that Jesus did not want this new person to be neglected any more than Jesus wanted His disciples to neglect Him. He sent a person who is totally committed to glorifying Him. He sent His Holy Spirit.

The Holy Spirit's office is to bring Jesus to us. This brings glory to Jesus. He does not want to take us away from Jesus. Does it glorify Jesus for Him to pay the price for our healing and no one benefit from His sacrifice? Does it glorify Jesus for His blessings to be hidden away and never received? Who glories in this? The enemy does. He takes advantage of seemingly unfulfilled promises.

It is time to understand the office of the Holy Spirit and recognize His equality with Jesus Christ and God the Father. There is no time limit we contend with. It may be that for an extended time we need much of our focus to be on the Holy Spirit. Most Christians that I know are never taught to develop a relationship with Him. We need our spiritual eyes to open. We must understand just how much we need Him in our life.

Now the Lord is that Spirit:
and where the Spirit of the Lord is, there is liberty.
2 Corinthians 3:17

A very important truth of the Bible tells us who the Holy Spirit is. He is the LORD.

Do we really consider the Holy Spirit as LORD? This consideration is foreign to many Christians. Mostly, He is thought to only inhabit our heart. Christians generally overlook His role in the Trinity and often refer to Him with an inappropriate characterization of *it*. Very few Christians appear to honor the Holy Spirit. We honor Him as we meet Him as LORD and embrace His LORDship.

Each time we read the word LORD in the Bible, we can think of the Holy Spirit. This is who He is. It makes a difference in our Christian life when we see Him in this way. He is no less LORD than Jesus Christ or God the Father. He is not a ghost. He is the LORD. He is not just a helper. He is the LORD and He helps us. He is not just a comforter. He is the LORD and He comforts us. He is not just a guide. He is the LORD and He guides us. He is the LORD and He is the One who makes our answered prayers evident to us. He is the LORD and He is here with us!

But the Holy Spirit will come and help you, because the Father will send the Spirit to take my place.
John 14:26 (CEV)

Chapter 2
HE SHALL RECEIVE OF MINE

*He shall glorify me: for he shall receive of mine, and shall **shew** it unto you. All things that the Father hath are mine: therefore said I, that he shall take of mine, and shall **shew** it unto you. John 16:14–15*

Shew in the King James Version of the Bible is the British variation of the word show. In the Greek, *shew* is *anaggello*, which means to declare, show, report, speak or tell. Within the context of John 16:14–15, the appropriate definition for *shew* is to declare or show. Merriam-Webster's Collegiate® Dictionary defines declare as *to make evident: show.** This definition of declare, in the sense of show, fits the meaning of *shew*.

> *He shall glorify me: for he shall receive of mine, and shall shew (make evident) it unto you. All things that the Father hath are mine: therefore said I, that he shall take of mine, and shall shew (make evident) it unto you. (Meaning of shew added in parenthesis)*

These verses explain how we receive from God. We receive all things of God from the Holy Spirit. Only the Holy Spirit receives all things from Jesus. A summation of these verses is shown on the following page.

All things that the Father hath are mine

God the Father has given all things to Jesus Christ.

For he shall receive of mine

The Holy Spirit receives all things from Jesus Christ.

And shall shew (make evident) it unto you

The Holy Spirit makes evident to us all things Jesus Christ received from God the Father.

Other Bible versions show a similar translation of John 16:14–15. The underlying principle is that the Holy Spirit makes every blessing of Jesus Christ evident to us here.

*He will bring glory to me by taking from what is mine and **making it known to you**. All that belongs to the Father is mine. That is why I said the Spirit will take from what is mine and **make it known to you**. (NIV)*

*He will honor me; he will take from me and **deliver it to you**. Everything the Father has is also mine. That is why I've said, 'He takes from me and **delivers to you**.' (THE MESSAGE)*

*He will bring me glory by **revealing to you** whatever he receives from me. All that the Father has is mine; this is what I mean when I say that the Spirit will **reveal to you** whatever he receives from me. (NLT)*

*He will honor and glorify Me, because He will take of (receive, draw upon) what is Mine and will **reveal (declare, disclose, transmit) it to you.** Everything that the Father has is Mine. That is what I meant when I said that He [the Spirit] will take the things that are Mine and will **reveal (declare, disclose, transmit) it to you***. (AMPLIFIED)

> *...for he shall receive of mine,*
> *and shall shew it unto you. John 16:14*

Many examples in the New Testament tell of believers who did everything they could to get to Jesus. We too would do this if only we knew how. Jesus is currently in heaven and seated at the right hand of God the Father. How can we get to Him? The real question is who will bring Jesus to us? The Holy Spirit does. We know this from John 16:14–15. He connects us individually to Jesus. I picture the Holy Spirit holding my hand here on earth and reaching His other hand up to heaven to hold the hand of Jesus. It is now, and only now, that we can receive the blessings of God. This is how vital the Holy Spirit is within the Trinity. The office of the Holy Spirit is no less vital for the Christian than the offices of God the Father and Jesus Christ.

It is not as difficult to get to Jesus as the enemy tells us. We find Jesus as we develop a relationship with the Holy Spirit and seek to stay close to Him. He provides the necessary union with Jesus that permits us to receive His blessings.

Even the Spirit of truth; whom the world cannot receive,
because it seeth him not, neither knoweth him: ...
John 14:17

Union with the Holy Spirit requires us to overcome an obstacle experienced by the world. We will not see the Holy Spirit. At first, we may not think He is present with us. Jesus said this is why the world could not receive the Spirit of truth. The world cannot see Him, so the world does not know He is here. The Christian who knows the Holy Spirit personally is not this carnally minded. Seeing Him is not required for us to recognize His presence. He is a person we recognize in spite of not seeing Him.

Suppose the Holy Spirit were standing across the street with His hands full of blessings from Jesus. Would it benefit us if we were standing on the opposite side of the street? No, there would be no benefit at all. Blessings are received when we abide with the Holy Spirit. He is in control of giving us these blessings. We simply strive to stay in union with Him. A relationship is the way to accomplish this.

For we wrestle not against flesh and blood,
but against principalities, against powers, against
the rulers of the darkness of this world, against
spiritual wickedness in high places. Ephesians 6:12

The words *high places* are from the Greek word *epouranios*, which means *above the sky, celestial, (in) heaven (-ly), high.* Satan's demonic hierarchy is located here. In the past, this demonic realm could interfere with what was given from heaven. Daniel's answered prayer from heaven was delayed for twenty one days because of this demonic realm. The angel Gabriel describes this realm of opposition in Daniel 10:12–13.

> *Then said he unto me, Fear not, Daniel: for from the first day that thou didst set thine heart to understand, and to chasten thyself before thy God, thy words were heard, and **I am come for thy words**. But the prince of the kingdom of Persia withstood me one and twenty days: but, lo, Michael, one of the chief princes, came to help me; and I remained there with the kings of Persia.*

Jesus dealt an enormous defeat to satan in his realm of opposition. He sent the Holy Spirit to live in us and dwell with us. Now, the Holy Spirit is our connection to the blessings of Jesus. His union with Jesus is infinitely stronger than any interference satan can produce. The Holy Spirit is in eternal union with Jesus. This demonic realm between heaven and earth can no longer delay blessings from reaching us. Blessings are now found in the Holy Spirit. The kingdom of God is in Him. He brings the riches of heaven to earth.

> *for the kingdom of God is not eating and drinking, but righteousness and peace and joy in the Holy Spirit.*
> *Romans 14:17 (NKJV)*

The riches of Jesus make up the kingdom of God. We find this kingdom on earth in only one place. This kingdom is within the Holy Spirit.

*And it shall come to pass in the last days, saith God, I will pour **out of** my Spirit upon all flesh: and your sons and your daughters shall prophesy, and your young men shall see visions, and your old men shall dream dreams: And on my servants and on my handmaidens I will pour **out** in those days **of** my Spirit; and they shall prophesy: Acts 2:17–18*

When we read these verses, we may think God will pour out the Holy Spirit, but this is not what the verses say. Our Father will instead be pouring out of what is within the Holy Spirit. Romans 14:17 tells us the kingdom of God is in Him.

The last days will supply a great outpouring from the kingdom of God within the Holy Spirit. This great outpouring of riches will be most prominent in those who know the Holy Spirit personally. Those who do not know Him will be entering this time with no experience of learning and understanding His ways. The Holy Spirit has a great deal to teach each of us. He teaches us how to take giant steps forward in our Christian life. He reveals what we never knew before. A relationship now will mean every-thing then. These days are upon us.

THE TRINITY

For of him, and through him, and to him,
are all things: ... Romans 11:36

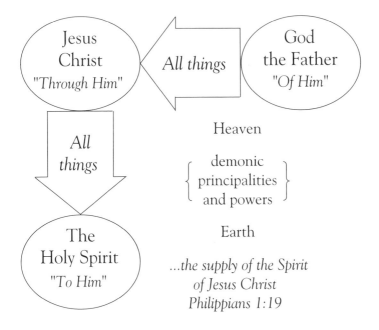

This illustration shows where spiritual blessings now reside. All things are inherent to the Holy Spirit living with us here. We will find all of our answered prayers in Him. His union with Jesus has brought everything to earth.

This pictorial follows closely with what John 16:14–15 shows us (see visual on receiving). The same terminology is also used.

All things originate in God the Father. All things always pass through Jesus Christ. All things are given to the Holy Spirit here on the earth. Each member of the Trinity is just as necessary as the other members. Each member is required for the Trinity to function as the Trinity. Each member of the Trinity has a unique role to play within the Trinity.

The demonic realm shown between heaven and earth is indicative of satan's defeat. This realm can no longer delay our answered prayers from heaven. The principalities and powers cannot interfere in the union of Jesus and the Holy Spirit. This tremendous defeat to satan has nullified much of his influence to affect us. All he can do now is attempt to interfere in the union we have with the Holy Spirit.

All things have now come to earth. The Holy Spirit lives with us here. This is why union with Him is so important. This is what is missing in the lives of so many Christians. This is what has hindered Christians in receiving from God. All we ask for is already here in the person of God the Holy Spirit. He lives with us here to make evident everything Jesus accomplished on the cross. As the Spirit of Jesus Christ, He holds everything we desire.

...and the supply of the Spirit of Jesus Christ,
Philippians 1:19

ASKING

For through him we both have access
by one Spirit unto the Father. Ephesians 2:18

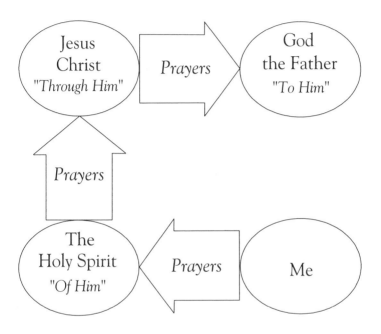

Access to God the Father is only through Jesus Christ. Access to Jesus Christ is only by the Holy Spirit. This is why the Holy Spirit is so important in our prayer life. The Holy Spirit places our prayers into the union of the Trinity. He enables our prayers to go through Jesus Christ and then to our Father. He ensures that our prayers are heard.

Effective prayer will always include the Holy Spirit. We can ask the Holy Spirit to give us the words to pray and He will do this. He knows areas needing prayer that we would never consider. We can ask Him to anoint our prayers. We can always invite and welcome the Holy Spirit into our prayer time. One of the Holy Spirit's names is the Spirit of supplications. He is the Holy Spirit of earnest prayer. He alone makes prayer in the Spirit possible. Leaving the Holy Spirit out of our prayer life is like not praying at all. We need to include Him.

RECEIVING

He shall glorify me: for he shall receive of mine, and shall shew (make evident) it unto you. All things that the Father hath are mine: therefore said I, that he shall take of mine, and shall shew (make evident) it unto you. John 16:14–15

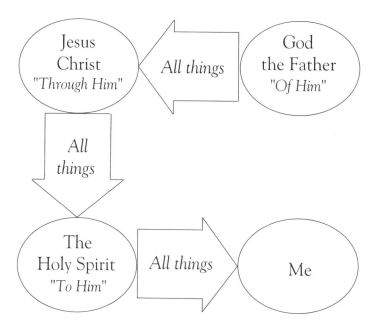

This illustration makes it easy to see how we receive from God. It is the same as the Trinity pictorial with Me added. God the Father gives all things to Jesus. Jesus gives all things to the Holy Spirit. The Holy Spirit makes all things evident to me.

All things originate in God the Father. All things pass through Jesus Christ. All things are received by the Holy

Spirit. The Holy Spirit is on earth with me. The Holy Spirit makes all things evident to me here.

With the Holy Spirit on the earth, it is logical that He would receive everything from Jesus in heaven. He can then make everything given by our Father evident to us here. When we understand John 16:14–15, we understand a facet of the Holy Spirit's office. We will receive only from the Holy Spirit.

Blessings and answered prayers are not obtainable without the Trinity functioning as the Trinity. Each member operates in a unique role. The Holy Spirit's role is receiving from Jesus and making His blessings and answered prayers evident to us here. When we neglect Him, the blessings can mostly remain within Him. Our relationship with the Holy Spirit largely determines this. When our relationship and union with the Holy Spirit is intact and developed, the way opens for receiving these blessings. It is like opening a door. If we spend time with Him and draw close to Him, the door opens. If we neglect Him, the door can remain mostly closed.

This visual also shows what is finished and what is yet to be completed. Our Father giving all to Jesus is completed. Jesus giving all to the Holy Spirit is finished also. Receiving from the Holy Spirit is not completed. This last act involves us and our union with the Holy Spirit. A relationship with the Holy Spirit allows Him to lead us to the place where we can receive. A relationship with the Holy Spirit also creates a new and separate union that is not there when there is no relationship. This new union permits us to live in and with the Holy Spirit. It is a union of love.

> *And I say unto you, Ask, and **it** shall be given you; seek,*
> *and Ye shall find; knock, and **it** shall be opened unto*
> *you. For every one that asketh receiveth; and he that*
> *seeketh findeth; and to him that knocketh **it** shall be*
> *opened. Luke 11:9–10*

This typical translation is what we are used to reading in our Bibles. What we have always read and understood from these verses has most likely omitted the intended instructtion of Jesus. Shown below is a better understanding of His teaching.

> *And I say unto you, Ask, and **HE** shall be given you;*
> *seek, and ye shall find; knock, and **HE** shall be opened*
> *unto you. For every one that asketh receiveth; and he*
> *that seeketh findeth; and to him that knocketh **HE** shall*
> *be opened. Luke 11:9–10*

The pronoun *he* is an accurate translation used in these verses. The Greek passive verbs for *given* and *opened* are third person singular and are not marked for grammatical gender. If the person of the Holy Spirit were considered as the subject of these verbs, the pronoun *he* could accurately be used.

Unfortunately, the pronoun *it* is accurate also. The word *Spirit* in Greek is grammatically neuter and is often referred to with a neuter pronoun. In our language, we would not associate personality with these pronouns. Although this translation is accurate, it is difficult to recognize the person of the Holy Spirit as the subject of these verbs.

A careful study of Luke 11:9–13 demonstrates the Holy Spirit to be the subject of Luke 11:9–10. In verse 9, Jesus instructs His disciples to ask. He says asking results in being given to. He informs them what to ask for in verse 13. The Holy Spirit is given to them that ask. Jesus was clearly referring to the Holy Spirit.

> *If ye then, being evil, know how to give good gifts unto your children: how much more shall your heavenly Father give the Holy Spirit to them that ask him?*
> *Luke 11:13*

When we consider the Holy Spirit as the subject of Luke 11:9–10, we truly find words of life giving revelation. Jesus tells us to ask for the Holy Spirit. He tells us to seek the Holy Spirit. He tells us to knock and the Holy Spirit will be opened to us. What is within the Holy Spirit? Romans 14:17 tells us the kingdom of God is within Him.

The actual meaning of Luke 11:9–10 is one of the greatest truths we will ever acquire from the Bible. Jesus tells us how to receive from God. His directive for receiving is asking for and seeking the Holy Spirit. When we are close enough to touch Him, then we may knock. Knocking requires contact. We cannot knock if we are far away from Him. We must come into His presence.

The Holy Spirit reveals Himself only to those who desire Him. This is why we must ask for Him. If we do not desire His person, He will not overrule our desires. Our God of love allows us to make the choice of desiring Him or not. If we do desire Him, we will receive Him. If we seek Him, we will find Him. If we gently knock, His kingdom opens to blessings in all things.

for the kingdom of God is not eating and drinking,
but righteousness and peace and joy in the Holy Spirit.
Romans 14:17 (NKJV)

Understanding who the kingdom of God is helps us to receive this kingdom. The kingdom of God in the Holy Spirit is righteousness, peace and joy. Who is righteousness, peace and joy? Jesus is.

In his days Judah shall be saved, and Israel shall dwell
safely: and this is his name whereby he shall be called,
THE LORD OUR RIGHTEOUSNESS.
Jeremiah 23:6

For he is our peace, who hath made both one, and hath
broken down the middle wall of partition between us;
Ephesians 2:14

These things have I spoken unto you, that my joy might
remain in you, and that your joy might be full.
John 15:11

Jesus is our righteousness, peace and our joy. When we understand that Jesus is the kingdom of God within the Holy Spirit, our love for Jesus will permit us to pray a prayer of love. When we ask for the kingdom of God, we will be asking for Jesus. This is a prayer our Father can say yes to. Just as God the Father will say yes to our request for the Holy Spirit, He will also answer yes to our request for Jesus, the kingdom of God.

...for he dwelleth with you, and shall be in you. John 14:17

Each time we receive from our Father, the Holy Spirit brings us the blessing. This imparting is by the Holy Spirit who dwells with us. His person inside our heart is for an additional purpose. He is there for our relationship with Jesus. He lives in our heart to open our heart. He provides our love for Jesus.

We are mistaken if we believe we can forget the Holy Spirit and still easily receive from God. This is what many Christians do. Most Christians realize the Holy Spirit lives within them, but do not understand the need to meet this same person on their outside. This is the reason why many find it so difficult to receive from God. They were never taught to know the One who dwells with us. The person of the Holy Spirit that we live with requires a relationship with us. The union in this relationship allows us to receive the kingdom of God from within Him.

Chapter 3
JESUS CHRIST—ALL THINGS

*For in him dwelleth all the fulness
of the Godhead bodily. Colossians 2:9*

When we think of Jesus, we usually picture Him in our mind as we see Him in the Gospels. We often think of Jesus as the humble servant of God willing to die for humanity. Today, Jesus is different. When Jesus died on the cross, His role as the sacrificial lamb was fulfilled. When Jesus was resurrected from the dead, He changed. He is no longer the Jesus we see in the Gospels. He has again taken His place beside God the Father in heaven. He has again regained the fullness of the Godhead. He is now everything we need.

> *His head and his hairs were white like wool, as white as snow; and his eyes were as a flame of fire; And his feet like unto fine brass, as if they burned in a furnace; and his voice as the sound of many waters. And he had in his right hand seven stars: and out of his mouth went a sharp two-edged sword: and his countenance was as the sun shineth in his strength. And when I saw him, I fell at his feet as dead. … Revelation 1:14–17*

The apostle John describes the resurrected Jesus and clearly portrays a picture of who Jesus is today. John knew Jesus personally and would have recognized Him. Yet, when he saw Jesus, he fell to the ground as a dead man. He was astonished to see this person of Jesus.

Paul also writes about the Jesus of today. When Jesus came to Paul, His awesome presence caused Paul to fall to the ground also. His presence caused Paul to immediately surrender. The brightness of Jesus caused Paul to lose his sight for three days. The encounter caused Paul such astonishment that he could not eat or drink for three days.

And as he journeyed, he came near Damascus: and suddenly there shined round about him a light from heaven: And he fell to the earth, and heard a voice saying unto him, Saul, Saul, why persecutest thou me? And he said, Who art thou, Lord? And the Lord said, I am Jesus whom thou persecutest: it is hard for thee to kick against the pricks. And he trembling and astonished said, Lord, what wilt thou have me to do? And the Lord said unto him, Arise, and go into the city, and it shall be told thee what thou must do. And the men which journeyed with him stood speechless, hearing a voice, but seeing no man. And Saul arose from the earth; and when his eyes were opened, he saw no man: but they led him by the hand, and brought him into Damascus. And he was three days without sight, and neither did eat nor drink. Acts 9:3–9

… And the city had no need of the sun, neither of the moon, to shine in it: for the glory of God did lighten it, and the Lamb is the light thereof. Revelation 21:22–23

It is difficult to grasp an understanding of the person of Jesus. All we comprehend of Him is not fully understood. The person of Jesus Christ is outside our limited realm of comprehension.

When we consider a person so full of light that the sun is not necessary, we accurately see the person of Jesus. He is light. Within the light of His person are His attributes. His attributes are His person. Within Him is life, wisdom and understanding, truth, faith, power, love, counsel and might, grace, knowledge, judgment, and holiness. These attributes of His person are the riches of His glory. These attributes are His Spirit. These attributes of Himself are the Holy Spirit.

> *... that I should preach among the Gentiles*
> *the unsearchable riches of Christ; Ephesians 3:8*

The unsearchable riches of Jesus are the person described in the book of the Revelation and the book of Acts. This person is the fullness of the Godhead. This is who Jesus is today.

The Holy Spirit is here to bring these riches to each Christian. He is here to impart to us the attributes of Christ. To do this, we must grant Him a portion of our focus and love. Access to the riches of Christ is found in our relationship and resulting union with the Holy Spirit. He joins us with Jesus in heaven.

> *All things that the Father hath are mine: therefore said I, that he*
> *shall take of mine, And shall shew it unto you. John 16:15*

The following chapters list twelve unsearchable riches of Jesus Christ. These unsearchable attributes of Jesus are actually names of the Holy Spirit. An understanding of the Trinity as described in John 16:15 tells us how these unsearchable riches become ours.

When the Holy Spirit comes to impart life to us, He is known as the Spirit of life. Jesus is the life He imparts. Life is one of the unsearchable riches of Jesus. When the Holy Spirit imparts power to us, He is now known as the Spirit of power. The power He imparts is also an attribute of Jesus. Power is another of these unsearchable riches. The name of the Holy Spirit tells us what attribute of Jesus He has received and what attribute He will impart to us. Jesus Christ is the subject of the Holy Spirit's name. The Holy Spirit is the Spirit of Jesus Christ.

God the Father is also the subject of these names of the Holy Spirit. It is appropriate that if God the Father has given all things to Jesus then scripture would confirm the unsearchable riches are also of Him. The Holy Spirit is not only the Spirit of Jesus Christ, but also the Spirit of God the Father. Each member of the Trinity is represented in these twelve unsearchable riches.

These names of the Holy Spirit are also the keys that open the kingdom of God to us here. Each of His names unlocks righteousness, peace or joy in our life.

> *for the kingdom of God is not eating and drinking,*
> *but righteousness and peace and joy in the Holy Spirit.*
> *Romans 14:17 (NKJV)*

Chapter 4
LIFE

…I am come that they might have life, and that they might have it more abundantly. John 10:10

GOD THE FATHER

*For as **the Father hath life** in himself; so hath he given to the Son to have life in himself; John 5:26*

GOD THE SON

*Jesus said unto her, **I am** the resurrection, and **the life**: he that believeth in me, though he were dead, yet shall he live: John 11:25*

GOD THE HOLY SPIRIT

*For the law of **the Spirit of life** in Christ Jesus hath made me free from the law of sin and death. Romans 8:2*

The accomplishments of Jesus on the cross qualify every Christian for His abundant life. His abundant life was shown to us in His resurrection. Only abundant life can resurrect the dead. Life is the person of Jesus Christ.

If we should be experiencing death or lack in any form, the life of Jesus is our remedy. When we need the life that only He is, we really should not seek this life. We should seek Him. Jesus can only give life as He gives of Himself. He is life.

And this is life eternal,
that they might know thee the only true God,
and Jesus Christ, whom thou hast sent. John 17:3

The prayer of Jesus defines eternal life as knowing God. We are not required to wait to experience eternal life. Eternal life can be ours now. We have the opportunity to know the person of God before we live in heaven. The person of God the Holy Spirit lives with us here and He offers this to us now. We can meet Him, know Him and enjoy Him. He is the Spirit of life.

For the law of the Spirit of life in Christ Jesus hath
made me free from the law of sin and death. Romans 8:2

Romans 8:2 gives us one of the many names of the Holy Spirit. The Holy Spirit is the Spirit of life. Notice where life is found in this verse. Life is found in Christ Jesus. Paul, however, received this life from the Holy Spirit. The Holy Spirit of life received life from Jesus and made this life evident to Paul. Paul then experienced freedom from sin and death.

Jesus not only embodies spiritual life, but His resurrection life is also for our physical body. I had been seeking Jesus for several weeks. I was asking for Him to visit me. One Sunday night as I was sleeping, I was awakened by the awesome presence of the Holy Spirit. I immediately felt billions of cells in my chest being powerfully reenergized with new life. It seemed that He was not creating new life, but that life was actually being transferred to me from Him. As this was happening, I began saying aloud, "Jesus is LORD! Jesus is LORD! Jesus is LORD!" By the end of the third exclamation, I could not bear the encounter any longer and His transferring of life stopped. The experience was so incredibly powerful. It was the most awesome experience of my life. The Holy Spirit of life made the life of Jesus evident to me.

...to another the gifts of healing by the same Spirit;
1 Corinthians 12:9

Life will only be imparted to us by the Holy Spirit. Jesus will not be doing it. He is the life. God the Father will not be doing it either. He has given all to Jesus. The Holy Spirit alone holds the office of imparting life. He will never claim to be this life. He made it clear in scripture that Jesus is life. Jesus also made it clear in John 16:14–15 who makes His life evident to us.

So many of us ask God to heal our bodies. How often do we include the Holy Spirit in the process of seeking this life from God? Should we leave out the person who will impart the new life we ask for? The Holy Spirit has been forgotten for too long. We must recognize our need to include Him. He is the third member of the Trinity that always functions as a Trinity. We must remember the way that God blesses us with new life—

>...*Not by might, nor by power, but by my spirit, saith the Lord of hosts. Zechariah 4:6*

———∞———

The life God gives is joy unspeakable

GOD'S KINGDOM OF JOY
*for **the kingdom of God is** not eating and drinking, but righteousness and peace and **joy** in the Holy Spirit. Romans 14:17 (NKJV)*

You will show me the way of life, granting me the joy of your presence and the pleasures of living with you forever. Psalm 16:11 (NLT)

RECEIVING LIFE

He shall glorify me: for he shall receive of mine, and shall shew (make evident) it unto you. All things that the Father hath are mine: therefore said I, that he shall take of mine, and shall shew (make evident) it unto you. John 16:14–15 (Meaning of shew added in parenthesis)

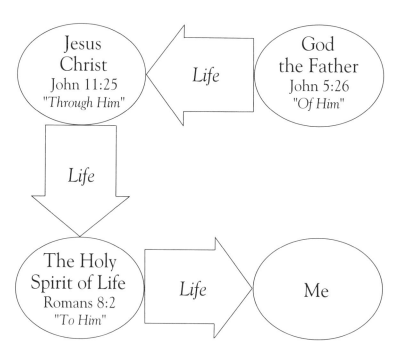

PROMISE

...according to the promise of life
which is in Christ Jesus, 2 Timothy 1:1

THE HOLY SPIRIT
...in whom also after that ye believed, ye were sealed
*with that **holy Spirit of promise**, Ephesians 1:13*

Life is the primary promise of the Bible. All of God's promises are a portion of the life we find in Jesus Christ.

Every promise of life we find legitimately belongs to God's children. The Holy Spirit of promise designates us as recipients. Jesus seals us with the Holy Spirit of promise. He seals us as belonging to God. This is a literal seal. He seals us on our forehead.

> *Saying, Hurt not the earth, neither the sea, nor the trees, till we have sealed the servants of our God in their foreheads. Revelation 7:3*

> *And thou shalt make a plate of pure gold, and grave upon it, like the engravings of a signet, HOLINESS TO THE LORD. And thou shalt put it on a blue lace, that it may be upon the mitre; upon the forefront of the mitre it shall be. And it shall be upon Aaron's forehead, that Aaron may bear the iniquity of the holy things, which the children of Israel shall hallow in all their holy gifts; and it shall be always upon his forehead, that they may be accepted before the LORD. Exodus 28:36–38*

When I first met the Holy Spirit, He began allowing me to feel His seal. I would often feel a certain numbness and presence on my forehead. With His seal was the understanding that this was from Him. He taught me through scripture what I was feeling.

It is always a very special occasion when He grants the awareness of His seal. Nothing gives more assurance and peace. Every true believer has received His seal whether felt or not. But it is always a special blessing for Him to allow us to feel it.

> *…Now if any man have not the Spirit of Christ,*
> *he is none of his. Romans 8:9*

The seal of the Holy Spirit is our first step to receiving God's promises. Before we can receive from God, we must be qualified to receive from Him. We must be His. The seal of the Holy Spirit of promise qualifies us as belonging to God. We become the children of God.

> *For all the promises of God in him are yea,*
> *and in him Amen, unto the glory of God by us.*
> *2 Corinthians 1:20*

The next step to receiving the promises of God is to be approved for these blessings. Our union with Jesus Christ brings the approval we need. Each promise has the words *yes* and *Amen* assigned to them. This approval is reserved for those who belong to Him. The children of God will find complete approval for every promise of God. The Greek word *Amen* is defined as firm, trustworthy, surely and verily.

*And if ye be Christ's, then are ye Abraham's seed,
and heirs according to the promise. Galatians 3:29*

Romans 8:9 declares that when we receive the Holy Spirit we belong to Jesus. When we belong to Jesus, Galatians 3:29 tells us we are Abraham's seed and heirs according to the promise. The promise God made to Abraham is our promise also.

For when God made promise to Abraham, because he could swear by no greater, he sware by himself, Saying, Surely blessing I will bless thee, and multiplying I will multiply thee. Hebrews 6:13–14

God initiated an irreversible promise of blessing to Abraham and his seed. God was so emphatic in His promise that He made it only possible to bless Abraham. He made all that is within Him, available to Abraham and the heirs of His promise.

*...and the Lord had blessed Abraham in all things.
Genesis 24:1*

Blessings in all things belong to the child of God. Jesus has already approved these blessings in all things. Blessings in all things comprise blessings as unlimited as God is. There is nothing omitted. This truthfully belongs to every Christian. It begins with the seal of the Holy Spirit. His union with Jesus has provided the approval we need. It ends with the Holy Spirit also. We will receive these blessings from Him.

All things that the Father hath are mine:
therefore said I, that he shall take of mine,
and shall shew (make evident) it unto you. John 16:15

Union with the Holy Spirit is the way we receive from God. We can see what our union with the Holy Spirit provides from Romans 8:9. He produces our union with Jesus Christ. His union with Jesus brings us blessings in all things. Jesus accomplished everything for us. The Holy Spirit manifests what Jesus accomplished.

The all things referred to in Genesis 24:1 are the same all things referred to in John 16:15. All things are all things. These blessings in all things have now been given to Jesus from God the Father. As these blessings pass through Jesus, He attaches the declarations of *yes* and *Amen* to them for His children. These blessings are then given to the Holy Spirit. The Holy Spirit will make the promised blessings in all things evident to us here.

The world cannot receive these blessings in all things. There is no union to produce this for them. The world, instead, concentrates on substitutes. Worldly pleasures are all that is left. The blessings of God include pleasure beyond what material pleasures provide. God's blessings always include life. The life He provides is beyond our natural perception of life. Meaningful, fulfilling, delightful life is provided in His blessings. There is no substitute for Him and what He gives. Jesus changes ordinary life into supernatural life. Jesus turns water into wine.

*That the blessing of Abraham might come on the
Gentiles through Jesus Christ; that we might receive
the promise of the Spirit through faith. Galatians 3:14*

*…and you shall receive the gift of the Holy Spirit.
"For the promise is to you and to your children, …
Acts 2:38–39 (NKJV)*

These verses show the union of the Holy Spirit with the
blessings of Abraham. The Holy Spirit is here with us now
and He contains these blessings in all things. Since the
Holy Spirit has been sent to earth with all these blessings,
would it not follow that a relationship with Him would be
vital? The blessings begin to become evident as we desire
the Holy Spirit as a person and our relationship is intact.
Our new union with the Holy Spirit is found in our
relationship with Him. We must remember that He is a
person. How can we ever hope to have union with this
person if we neglect Him? Our all important union with the
Holy Spirit is dependent on us.

The Holy Spirit comes to us many times and we
regretfully ignore Him. How often He has desired to bless
us only to have us say no to Him. When we neglect Him,
we say no to His blessings. The Holy Spirit needs our
attention. Part of our faith is our focus, and He comes to us
by faith. If we will say yes to Him by focusing on Him when
He does come to us, He can impart to us. The problem is
that we know little of the Holy Spirit's ways. We often may
not realize how gentle He is. His gentleness is His love and
He only acts in love. He always gives everything in love. He
is not only the Spirit of promise, but also the Holy Spirit of
love.

PARTAKING OF LIFE

As the living Father hath sent me, and I live by the Father: so he that eateth me, even he shall live by me. John 6:57

Artos, *ar'tos*; from Greek (airo); *bread (as raised) or a loaf.*
Airo, *ah'ee–ro*; a primary verb; *to lift.*

> *For I have received of the Lord that which also I delivered unto you, That the Lord Jesus the same night in which he was betrayed took bread: And when he had given thanks, he brake it, and said, Take, eat: this is my body, which is broken for you: this do in remembrance of me. After the same manner also he took the cup, when he had supped, saying, This cup is the new testament in my blood: this do ye, as oft as ye drink it, in remembrance of me. 1 Corinthians 11:23–25*

The Passover meal eaten by Jesus and His disciples always included unleavened bread. Unleavened bread in the New Testament is the Greek word *azumos*.

The Greek word for the bread used in the LORD'S Supper is *artos*. *Artos* is from the Greek verb *airo*. These Greek words tell us the bread used in the LORD'S Supper was leavened bread or raised bread. In every scripture referring to the LORD'S Supper, the bread used is the Greek word *artos*.

When Jesus initiated the LORD'S Supper, He began by giving the disciples a broken loaf of raised bread. He said, "Take and eat, this (raised bread) is my body, which is broken for you." Jesus was introducing something new to the disciples.

...Take, eat: this is my body, which is broken for you: this do in remembrance of me. 1 Corinthians 11:24

When Jesus initiated the LORD'S Supper, He was giving instructions for a future time. He instructed the disciples to partake of His body in remembrance of Him. Essentially, Jesus was telling the disciples to partake of His body when He was no longer with them. This future time of partaking would be after His death on the cross and after His resurrection from the dead. It was after His resurrection that Jesus left the disciples and returned to heaven. This future time of partaking would provide the disciples with an important accomplishment of His death and resurrection— the glorified, resurrected and raised body of Jesus. Partaking of the raised body of Jesus complements Jesus giving raised bread *(artos)* to the disciples in the LORD'S Supper.

...This cup is the new testament in my blood: this do ye, as oft as ye drink it, in remembrance of me. 1 Corinthians 11:25

Jesus also made it apparent that the partaking of His blood was for a future time. He instructed the disciples to partake of His blood in remembrance of Him. This future time of partaking would be after Jesus returned to heaven. Only when Jesus was no longer with the disciples would the partaking of His blood be in remembrance of Him. This future time of partaking would provide another accomplishment of His death and resurrection. This future time of partaking would make available the blood accepted by His Father as the payment for the sin of the world. This blood is now in heaven with Jesus. This is the blood of the New Covenant.

For anyone who eats and drinks without recognizing the body of the Lord eats and drinks judgment on himself. That is why many among you are weak and sick, and a number of you have fallen asleep. 1 Corinthians 11:29–30 (NIV)

Discerning the LORD'S body in the LORD'S Supper is such an important issue. The Apostle Paul states that when we do not discern the body of Jesus in the LORD'S Supper we enter God's judgment. So the question arises as to whether viewing the LORD'S Supper as merely symbolic would qualify as discerning His body correctly. These verses do not mention symbols or representations. The seriousness of the subject communicates that we are to discern the actual body of Jesus Christ.

For my flesh is meat indeed, and my blood is drink indeed. John 6:55

I am the living bread which came down from heaven: if any man eat of this bread, he shall live forever: and the bread that I will give is my flesh, which I will give for the life of the world. The Jews therefore strove among themselves, saying, How can this man give us his flesh to eat? Then Jesus said unto them, Verily, verily I say unto you, Except ye eat the flesh of the Son of man, and drink his blood, ye have no life in you. John 6:51–53

Jesus makes no mention of symbols in His words either. He emphatically states that the bread is His flesh that He would give for the life of the world. He also expressly states that His flesh is meat indeed and His blood is drink indeed. How could He make a stronger statement? His flesh is to be eaten and His blood is to drink. What did the Jews say to this? They said what many Christians say today—"How can this man give us his flesh to eat?"

...I am the resurrection, and the life: ... John 11:25

Many believe the LORD'S Supper allows us to partake of the broken body of Jesus. The body of Jesus was broken 2000 years ago. His body has changed since then. He is now risen and resurrected. It is not possible to partake of His broken body that hung on the cross. That time has passed. We cannot partake of the past. The body of Christ is no longer paying the price for man's sin. The risen body of Jesus now contains resurrection life.

Jesus never desired for us to partake of His broken body. That is why He went to the cross in our place. He has never desired for us to partake of the suffering His broken body endured. His body was broken so our body would not be broken. The payment for our body is totally His. We cannot partake of His payment.

...seven days shalt thou eat unleavened bread therewith, even the bread of affliction; ... Deuteronomy 16:3

Unleavened bread is referred to as the bread of affliction. The bread of affliction is an appropriate name for the body of Jesus that hung on the cross. The broken body of Jesus was the payment for every sin of man and every curse that sin can produce. His broken body paid every penalty deserving to man. His broken body paid the price for new life in our body. The broken body of Jesus is the payment for our healing.

Who his own self bare our sins in his own body on the tree, that we, being dead to sins, should live unto righteousness: by whose stripes ye were healed.
1 Peter 2:24

And Jesus said unto them, I am the bread of life: …
John 6:35

The bread of life is the resurrected body of Jesus. It is interesting that *artos* is used in John 6:35. Jesus is describing Himself as a loaf of raised bread, full of life. This raised bread is what we partake of in the LORD's Supper. Life is the benefit of His resurrected body. He provides new life for our bodies and forgiveness of our sins as we partake of Him.

*When we ask the Lord's blessing upon our drinking from the **cup of wine** at the Lord's Table, this means, doesn't it, that all who drink it are sharing together **the blessing of Christ's blood**?*

*And when we break off pieces of the **bread from the loaf** to eat there together, this shows that we are sharing together in **the benefits of his body**.*
1 Corinthians 10:16 (TLB)

All things that the Father hath are mine:
therefore said I, that he shall take of mine,
and shall shew (make evident) it unto you. John 16:15

Does the Holy Spirit have access to the risen body of Jesus and to the blood of Jesus? Yes, Jesus and the Holy Spirit are always in perfect union. The risen, resurrected body and the New Covenant blood of Jesus are both in heaven. John saw the resurrected Jesus and His blood there when he visited heaven.

> *His eyes were as a flame of fire, and on his head were many crowns; and he had a name written, that no man knew, but he himself. And he was clothed with a vesture* **dipped in blood***: and his name is called The Word of God. Revelation 19:12–13*

As we partake of the LORD'S body and blood in the LORD'S Supper, the Holy Spirit is able to receive from Jesus (His risen body and blood currently in heaven) and make these benefits evident to us (John 16:15). He brings heaven to earth. His only union is in the resurrected and raised person of Jesus. He makes the resurrection life found in Jesus Christ evident to us as we recognize the LORD'S body and blood in our partaking.

At times the imparting of this new life will be felt while partaking. The Holy Spirit will allow us to perceive this. We should welcome and invite the Holy Spirit into our time of partaking. His union with Jesus and His union with us makes Him essential for receiving the benefits of the resurrected body and New Covenant blood of Jesus Christ.

> *For as often as ye eat this bread, and drink this cup,*
> *ye do shew the Lord's death till he come.*
> *1 Corinthians 11:26*

As often as we partake of the body and blood of Jesus, we show to God the Father, Jesus, the Holy Spirit, the angels, the devil and his demons, and to our flesh the accomplished work of the cross. We show to all that Jesus paid the price for every aspect of our life. His finished work on the cross includes the results of His sacrifice. New life for our bodies and forgiveness of sins are two of His accomplishments.

> *Ye cannot drink the cup of the Lord, and the cup of devils:*
> *ye cannot be partakers of the Lord's table,*
> *and of the table of devils. 1 Corinthians 10:21*

Partaking of the LORD'S Supper results in recognizable protection from our enemy. Even when the influences of the enemy come against us, we find that our spirit has become strong. Spiritual strength is a definite benefit of the LORD'S Supper. This is so important. When we receive new life from Jesus, this spiritual strength will be needed. The enemy will always attempt to steal what we receive from God. The strength of Jesus inside us will enable us to keep what God has given.

> *For anyone who eats and drinks without recognizing the*
> *body of the Lord eats and drinks judgment on himself. That*
> *is why many among you are weak and sick, and a number*
> *of you have fallen asleep. 1 Corinthians 11:29–30 (NIV)*

As we recognize the body and blood of Jesus in the LORD's Supper, we are imparted life by the Holy Spirit of life. If we do not recognize the LORD's body, the verses above tell us we enter God's judgment. The two thieves on either side of Jesus as He hung on the cross paint a picture of this. On one side of Jesus was the thief who recognized the body and blood of the person on the cross as being Jesus, the Son of God. He received life from God. On the

other side of Jesus was the thief who could not recognize
the body and blood of the person on the cross as being
Jesus, the Son of God. He did not receive this life. Today
we have the same discernment to make as the two thieves.

*I call heaven and earth to record this day against you,
that I have set before you life and death, blessing and
cursing: therefore choose life, that both thou and thy
seed may live: Deuteronomy 30:19*

Chapter 5
WISDOM AND UNDERSTANDING

*...and to desire that ye might be filled
with the knowledge of his will in all wisdom
and spiritual understanding; Colossians 1:9*

GOD THE FATHER

*With the ancient is **wisdom**; and in length of days **understanding**. With him is **wisdom** and strength, he hath counsel and **understanding**. Job 12:12–13*

GOD THE SON

*But unto them which are called, both Jews and Greeks, Christ the power of God, and **the wisdom of God**.
1 Corinthians 1:24*

*Counsel is mine, and sound wisdom: **I am understanding**; I have strength. Proverbs 8:14*

GOD THE HOLY SPIRIT

*And the spirit of the LORD shall rest upon him, **the spirit of wisdom and understanding**, the spirit of counsel and might, the spirit of knowledge and of the fear of the LORD; Isaiah 11:2*

The wisdom of the prudent is to understand his way: …
Proverbs 14:8

Understanding is present when we recognize which path God has for us to travel. Choosing His path reflects our measure of wisdom.

God's direction is the only path that brings fulfillment to our life. It is much easier to choose the correct path when we have a relationship with the Holy Spirit. He will lead us in the direction we are to travel. When we neglect the Holy Spirit, we are not allowing Him to lead us. If there is no relationship, He is hindered in conveying the wisdom to follow His leading.

As we travel His path, the Holy Spirit will be in front leading us. He will not be behind us pushing. He only leads. Sometimes there are obstacles in the path. With Him in front, He clears them away so we can go forward. This is why it is so important not to get ahead of Him. The path is not safe unless He goes first. He not only knows where we are going, but He clears away the obstacles.

The enemy has paths for us also. His paths can appear to be God's path. They are disguised to trick us. Wisdom prevents us from traveling these paths. Most often, we will feel pushed to go in these directions. If we feel this, we should not consider this a leading of the Holy Spirit. The Holy Spirit gently says, "Come this way with Me." The enemy says, "Go this way and do it NOW!" Wisdom recognizes the difference.

But the wisdom that is from above is first pure,
then peaceable, gentle, and easy to be intreated,
full of mercy and good fruits, without partiality,
and without hypocrisy. James 3:17

True qualities of wisdom are the personalities of Jesus Christ. When we see the Holy Spirit making these qualities evident in our life, He is developing our wisdom.

Pure
...even as he is pure. 1 John 3:3

Peaceable
For he is our peace, ... Ephesians 2:14

Gentle
...by the meekness and gentleness of Christ, ...
2 Corinthians 10:1

Easy to be intreated
For I came down from heaven, not to do mine own will,
but the will of him that sent me. John 6:38

Full of mercy
...that the Lord is very pitiful, and of tender mercy.
James 5:11

Full of good fruits
I am the vine, ye are the branches: He that abideth in
me, and I in him, the same bringeth forth much fruit: ...
John 15:5

Without partiality
> *...neither is there respect of persons with him.*
> *Ephesians 6:9*

Without hypocrisy
> *Who did no sin, neither was guile found in his mouth:*
> *1 Peter 2:22*

> *…Knowing God results in every other kind*
> *of understanding. Proverbs 9:10 (TLB)*

We will never adequately know God if we disregard the Holy Spirit. We may know a great deal about Him, but this is not the same as knowing Him. Knowing Him produces understanding beyond our knowledge of Him. Knowing our God produces spiritual understanding.

Knowing the Holy Spirit requires that we spend time with Him. Living life with Him produces understanding of His ways and desires. The only way we can ever understand a person is to spend time with that person.

A true relationship with the Holy Spirit also brings forth a sharing. It is a sharing between life in our realm and life in His realm of the Spirit. He steps into our realm and He allows us to step into His. This develops our spiritual understanding. This sharing is Spirit to spirit. This sharing feeds our spirit. Our yearning for the Holy Spirit is key to this growth. He feeds our spirit as we are hungry and thirsty for Him. Asking Him to increase our hunger keeps our sharing alive. This keeps us from becoming spiritually content. We are always to be longing for Him. Our hunger for the Holy Spirit is necessary for understanding Him.

...but they that seek the Lord
understand all things. Proverbs 28:5

Our desire to understand God's will requires us to seek the Holy Spirit. He will communicate to us the under-standing we desire. As we seek Him, our desires become voluntarily replaced with His desires. The only desire we hold to is Him. We want to find Him. We want to be with Him. We want to please Him. His direction becomes the direction we want.

It seems that the measure of our seeking Him is often the measure of His direction. When we intently seek Him, He seems to generously reveal to us. When we forget Him, we show Him we do not need His direction. His direction is dependent on our desire to seek Him.

One Sunday morning, I began crying out to God. I needed His direction in a particular matter. I did not know what to do. While intensely crying out and seeking His direction, He began to communicate to me. He imparted an understanding of His will. I immediately felt a burden to contact a pastor in Uganda. I clearly understood that He wanted me to initiate a crusade for the displaced refugees there. My original desire for direction from Him resulted in a new direction He wanted me to travel.

Fund raising efforts for the refugees began the same morning He communicated to me. Within five days, $5000 was collected and sent to the pastor in Uganda. He bought medicine, approximately 2000 blankets and many truck loads of food. The refugees were just returning to their ravaged homes when the supplies arrived. The rebels had stolen all of their possessions. It was the perfect time to arrive with provisions. Jesus stickers were on the truck and all the people bringing help wore Jesus T–shirts. There was no doubt who provided the relief. Jesus did.

During the relief effort, God granted a vision to me that revealed why the crusade was so important to Him. I saw the pastor standing beside a truckload of food, holding a little girl in his arms. He said, "Brother Gary, this is what the money was for." What a rewarding experience God's direction was.

———∞———

Wisdom and understanding follow God's path
resulting in a life of peace

GOD'S KINGDOM OF PEACE
*for **the kingdom of God is** not eating and drinking,*
*but righteousness and **peace** and joy in the Holy Spirit.*
Romans 14:17 (NKJV)

Happy is the man that findeth wisdom, and the man that getteth understanding. For the merchandise of it is better than the merchandise of silver, and the gain thereof than fine gold. She is more precious than rubies: and all the things thou canst desire are not to be compared unto her. Length of days is in her right hand; and in her left hand riches and honour. Her ways are ways of pleasantness, and all her paths are peace.
Proverbs 3:13–17

RECEIVING
WISDOM AND UNDERSTANDING

He shall glorify me: for he shall receive of mine, and shall shew (make evident) it unto you. All things that the Father hath are mine: therefore said I, that he shall take of mine, and shall shew (make evident) it unto you. John 16:14–15 (Meaning of shew added in parenthesis)

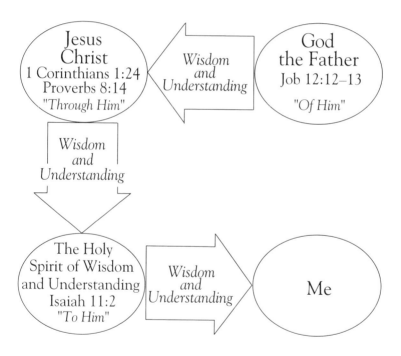

FEAR OF THE LORD

The fear of the Lord is the beginning of wisdom: Proverbs 9:10

THE HOLY SPIRIT

*And the spirit of the Lord shall rest upon him, the spirit of wisdom and understanding, the spirit of counsel and might, **the spirit** of knowledge and **of the fear of the Lord**;* Isaiah 11:2

The Holy Spirit will teach every Christian the wisdom of fearing God. We are to fear God and not lightly regard Him. Only the Christian knows this wisdom. The world is not concerned. The world does not fear Him, yet.

The struggle we encounter in life is our struggle with self. Our selfish nature always wants its way. Sometimes this selfish nature can attempt to gain a stronghold in our relationship with God. Without us realizing it, this nature can attempt to control God.

Many trials may be required to teach us that we are never permitted to direct or manipulate God. We can never force Him to give us what we desire. We are, instead, to ask of Him and then have faith in His love for us. If we should attempt to force God to answer our requests, we show Him that we do not fear Him. If we attempt to force God to do anything, we can be assured an adjustment is needed in our spiritual life.

Any attempt to control God establishes that a fresh understanding of Him is needed. Suffering accomplishes this change in attitude. The suffering we require seems to be reflective of how far away we have strayed. If we pull away from God when He says no to our desires, we will experience suffering and separation. If we quickly return to Him, our suffering will be minimal. If our reaction to His denial is more serious, our suffering will be more severe. The farther we pull away from God, the deeper our suffering will be. Our reaction to God's denial shows us how much we actually fear God and how much we are focused on our desires. The intended result of this painful trial should be a fresh revelation of who God is. The trial is necessary to change our perception of Him. God must sometimes show us that He is God and that we are not. He must sometimes remind us that we serve Him and that He does not serve us. When we recognize that His will is what matters and not our desires of Him, we come back into focus. He is an awesome God who requires those who love Him to fear and reverence Him. When the fear of God is restored in our life, we enter the place where He blesses us.

> *The secret of the Lord is with them that fear him;*
> *and he will shew them his covenant. Psalm 25:14*

It is no wonder the fear of the LORD is the beginning of wisdom. What a promise He makes to those who fear Him. When the fear of the LORD is present in our life, God's covenant will be made evident. Blessings in all things are the covenant God made with Abraham and his descendants. Christians are the children of this covenant. When the Holy Spirit teaches us to fear God, He is teaching us the beginning of wisdom. He teaches us this so He can impart the blessings of Abraham to us.

Our fear of God is a reflection of our relationship with Him. We fear God because we realize we can do nothing apart from Him. We cannot even pray without Him. We fear Him because we realize He keeps our relationship intact, not us. We fear Him because we continually fail Him and hurt Him. We fear Him because all decisions are ultimately His. We fear Him because when we cannot find Him, we experience the lack of all He is.

The Holy Spirit's concern for us requires Him to teach us the difficult lesson of fearing God. If we can recognize what He is teaching us, we are not as likely to rebel against Him. Even when our flesh does rebel, the understanding of what He is doing makes the suffering worthwhile. When the beginning of wisdom is within us, the benefits will also belong to us.

> *But unto you that fear my name shall the Sun of righteousness arise with healing in his wings; and ye shall go forth, and grow up as calves of the stall. And ye shall tread down the wicked; for they shall be ashes under the soles of your feet in the day that I shall do this, saith the Lord of hosts. Malachi 4:2–3*
>
> *He will fulfill the desire of them that fear him: …*
> *Psalm 145:19*

Chapter 6
TRUTH

*But I will shew thee that which is noted
in the scripture of truth: … Daniel 10:21*

GOD THE FATHER

*He is the Rock, his work is perfect: for all his ways are
judgment: **a God of truth** and without iniquity, just and
right is he. Deuteronomy 32:4*

GOD THE SON

*Jesus saith unto him, **I am** the way, **the truth**, and the
life: … John 14:6*

GOD THE HOLY SPIRIT

*But when the Comforter is come, whom I will send unto
you from the Father, even **the Spirit of truth**, which
proceedeth from the Father, he shall testify of me:
John 15:26*

Even the Spirit of truth (reality); whom the world cannot
receive, because it seeth him not, neither knoweth him:
but ye know him; for he dwelleth with you, and shall
be in you. John 14:17 (parenthesis added)*

* Greek 225, Strong's; *aletheia (al-ay'-thi-a)*; truth: true,
× truly, truth, verity.

The Greek word for truth, *aletheia*, also means verity or
reality. I believe this to be the meaning Jesus intended for
the Holy Spirit in John 14:17. What an appropriate name
for the Holy Spirit. He is the Spirit of reality.

Before I met the Holy Spirit, I had no idea that I could be
with God here. I had no idea that a holy God would allow
such a thing. I had numerous reasons formulated in my
mind that disqualified me from being with Him here. But
then I met Him and I learned that none of them mattered
to Him. Only my desire for Him mattered. It was my heart
that He wanted and not my self righteousness. I felt that I
was the only person on earth that knew this secret about
Him. And I wondered why I was never taught in church
that I could be with Him here.

I soon found the Holy Spirit to be much different from
what I saw in many churches that professed His reality. I
found Him so gentle. I found Him so Holy. I found Him so
loving and so intent in His desire to give Himself to me. In
Him, I found life. Life was being with Him. And I
understood that I was spending my time with a person, a
person I could not see, but a person I knew was there. I
could not wait for the workday to be over so I could go
home and be alone with Him. I had realized the reality of
God the Holy Spirit.

I also understood there could be no turning back with God. I could no longer claim I did not know God was real. But I never wanted to anyway. I experienced a depth of love I had never known with any other person. I found myself needing Him more and more. Now I knew what it was like to be with Him.

Only after I knew His reality could I recognize my years of stagnation as a Christian. I was a Christian that only knew of Him. I had always needed His reality to make my Christian walk real. Without His reality, I was dying. I knew no life in God. Only my beliefs were there before.

For many years, His reality caused me not to ask my Father for anything apart from His Holy Spirit. I would attend a church service and recognize that I only knew one prayer, my prayer of asking only for Him. During these years of asking only for the Holy Spirit, I experienced my greatest blessings, blessings that were never asked for. He already knew my desires. I learned that God will not only give us what we need, He will give us things we want. Big things. I learned that His first commandment provided for all my desires of Him.

His reality came to me in many ways. I first began feeling His seal on my forehead. I also began feeling His wonderful waves of cleansing and comfort, His anointing upon my hands, His touch and His presence. I began to discern what was of Him and what was not. For the first time in my life, I became a spiritual Christian. There was nothing in life that compared with Him. Old things fell away as unimportant. They offered me nothing. His person mattered now. Just being close to Him became the objective and focus of life.

All the paths of the Lord are mercy and truth
unto such as keep his covenant and his testimonies.
Psalm 25:10

Mercy and truth are joined together with God. How we need them both. His mercy is revealed in His truth. A good example of this is found in Psalm 41.

Blessed is he that considereth the poor: the LORD will deliver him in time of trouble. The LORD will preserve him, and keep him alive; and he shall be blessed upon the earth: and thou wilt not deliver him unto the will of his enemies. The LORD will strengthen him upon the bed of languishing: thou wilt make all his bed in his sickness. Psalm 41:1–3

The truth of God's concern for the poor is revealed in His mercy toward those who consider their needs. God promises to deliver us from the enemy as we care for the poor. The word *make* in verse three is the Hebrew word *haphak (haw-fak')* which means to change, overturn or return. God promises to deliver us from sickness as we consider the needs of the poor.

But the hour cometh, and now is, when the true worshippers
shall worship the Father in spirit and in truth:
for the Father seeketh such to worship him.
God is a Spirit: and they that worship him must
worship him in spirit and in truth. John 4:23–24

Worshipping our Father in the manner He desires will always include His Holy Spirit. Worshipping Him apart from the Holy Spirit is unacceptable. True worshippers will worship God in Spirit and in truth. Three times the Greek word *pneuma* (*pnyoo'-mah*) is used in these scriptures for our word *Spirit*. Jesus is communicating the importance of the Holy Spirit in our worship.

We will worship in Spirit as we worship the Holy Spirit. His equality within the Trinity qualifies Him for being worshipped. It is so easy and rewarding to worship Him. We give Him everything we have inside us. We ask Him to open our heart so we can worship Him. Rivers of love flow out to Him when He opens our heart.

The Holy Spirit always takes our eyes off Himself. As we worship the Holy Spirit, He will redirect our worship to Jesus. It is automatic. Before we realize it, we are now worshipping Jesus in Spirit and in truth. With our heart opened by the Holy Spirit, tremendous love and beautiful truth flow out to Jesus. Our spirit has been given the opportunity to express our deepest feelings. Our spirit is able to express true love as we worship Jesus through the Holy Spirit.

Our worship is ultimately directed to our Father. Our love for our Father is now made real as we worship Him in Spirit and in truth. Our worship has come by the Holy Spirit, through Jesus Christ and now to our Father. We now have access to Him. Our worship has reached Him. Our worship is acceptable to Him. True worship of our Father begins with the Holy Spirit.

For through him we both have access by one Spirit unto the Father. Ephesians 2:18

Howbeit when he, the Spirit of truth, is come,
he will guide you into all truth: for he shall not speak of himself;
but whatsoever he shall hear, that shall he speak:
and he will shew you things to come. John 16:13

Jesus refers to the Holy Spirit as a person seven times in John 16:13. His use of personal pronouns distinctly reveals this very important truth.

Jesus tells us the Holy Spirit of truth is our teacher and revealer of truth. He tenderly guides us into the truths of God. When He reveals truth to us, we will retain it. Truth then becomes meaningful to us. He is very much needed for this. It is the Holy Spirit who places truth into our heart. He also helps to keep them there. Without Him, truth is quickly stolen away.

The Holy Spirit also helps us recognize the lies of the enemy for what they are. He will register a check in our spirit when we are told things that are untrue or only partially true. He informs us that something is not right. We may not know what is wrong, but the discernment is present. When we feel this discernment, we should follow it. He will often reveal later what is wrong.

When we know the Holy Spirit as a person, we gain spiritual eyes that separate truth from lies. These spiritual eyes are not our own. They are His. Without Him, we are easily deceived. Satan makes his lies so believable. Today, more than any time in history, we need the Holy Spirit beside us. We need His eyes of truth. We need the Holy Spirit of truth active in our life.

*But I will shew thee that which is noted
in the scripture of truth: … Daniel 10:21*

Truth enables us to recognize the lies of the enemy. The enemy tells us we are worthless. God says we are important enough to die for. The enemy tells us our future is bleak. God tells us He is preparing a mansion for us. The enemy says God is angry with us. God instead shows He loves us.

We are continually told so many, many lies. How enlightening it is to read the Bible and discover the truths contained in it. No wonder satan hates the Bible. His lies become exposed. When his lies are exposed, they do not contain the power to hold us any longer.

One of the enlightening truths of God is how personal He is. As we spend time with Him, He reveals to us the loving, uncondemning, giving and long suffering person He is. His character is so far beyond our own. God is often portrayed as judgmental, legalistic and impersonal. The words of the Bible and a relationship with God the Holy Spirit reveal the truth concerning Him.

Truth is also the revelation of who Jesus Christ is. He is all things. The nature of Jesus Christ includes the following: life, truth, wisdom and understanding, faith, power, love, counsel and might, grace, knowledge, judgment, glory and holiness. These characteristics of His nature are keys that open the kingdom of God to us here.

Truth reveals the lies of the enemy
resulting in a life of peace

GOD'S KINGDOM OF PEACE
for the kingdom of God is *not eating and drinking,*
*but righteousness and **peace** and joy in the Holy Spirit.*
Romans 14:17 (NKJV)

May grace, mercy, and peace, which come from God
our Father and from Jesus Christ his Son, be with us
who live in truth and love. 2 John 1:3 (NLT)

People of Judah, I, the LORD, demand that whenever
you go without food as a way of worshiping me, it
should become a time of celebration. No matter if it's the
fourth month, the fifth month, the seventh month, or the
tenth month, you should have a joyful festival. So love
truth and live at peace. Zechariah 8:18 (CEV)

RECEIVING TRUTH

He shall glorify me: for he shall receive of mine, and shall shew (make evident) it unto you. All things that the Father hath are mine: therefore said I, that he shall take of mine, and shall shew (make evident) it unto you. John 16:14–15 (Meaning of shew added in parenthesis)

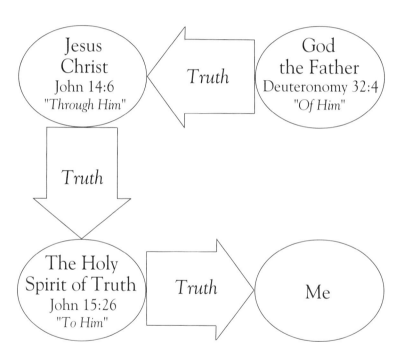

PROPHECY

——∞——

...even the Spirit of truth, which proceedeth
from the Father, he shall testify of me: John 15:26

THE HOLY SPIRIT

And I fell at his feet to worship him. And he said unto
me, See thou do it not: I am thy fellowservant, and of
thy brethren that have the testimony of Jesus: worship
God: for the testimony of Jesus is **the spirit of**
prophecy. *Revelation 19:10*

——∞——

The Holy Spirit of truth testifies the truths of Jesus into our heart. Our testimony of Jesus is formulated from these truths. Now these truths need to be told to the world. The spoken testimony of Jesus is the office of the Holy Spirit of prophecy. He enables us to speak our testimony in spite of opposition and consequences. This is one reason why the apostle John was exiled to the island of Patmos. His testimony of Jesus put him there.

> *I John, who also am your brother, and companion in*
> *tribulation, and in the kingdom and patience of Jesus*
> *Christ, was in the isle that is called Patmos, for the word*
> *of God, and for the testimony of Jesus Christ.*
> *Revelation 1:9*

Our testimony of Jesus enrages satan. Our testimony of Jesus exposes the truths of God and exposes satan as the liar that he is. The spoken testimony of Jesus contains spiritual light that makes it possible to see the truth. This too is the office of the Holy Spirit of prophecy.

> *And the dragon was wroth with the woman, and went to make war with the remnant of her seed, which keep the commandments of God, and have the testimony of Jesus Christ. Revelation 12:17*

Our testimony of Jesus also overcomes satan.

> *And they overcame him by the blood of the Lamb, and by the word of their testimony; and they loved not their lives unto the death. Revelation 12:11*

The testimony of Jesus is what is inside us. The words of Jesus are hidden in our heart. Who manifests them? The Spirit of prophecy does. He knows every truth of Jesus within us. He manifests the truths of Jesus in our spoken words.

The Holy Spirit of prophecy also gives us information for the future. Many times this will come in a dream or in a vision. Jesus knows the future just as well as He knows the present. When His words for the future are needed, Jesus will declare them to us. The Holy Spirit of prophecy brings His words to us.

> *We have also a more sure word of prophecy; whereunto ye do well that ye take heed, as unto a light that shineth in a dark place, until the day dawn, and the day star arise in your hearts: 2 Peter 1:19*

Chapter 7
FAITH

...but the just shall live by his faith. Habakkuk 2:4

GOD THE FATHER

*Know therefore that the LORD thy God, he is God, **the faithful God**, which keepeth covenant and mercy with them that love him and keep his commandments to a thousand generations; Deuteronomy 7:9*

GOD THE SON

*Looking unto Jesus **the author and finisher of** our **faith**; ... Hebrews 12:2*

GOD THE HOLY SPIRIT

*We having the same **spirit of faith**, according as it is written, I believed, and therefore have I spoken; we also believe, and therefore speak; Knowing that he which raised up the Lord Jesus shall raise up us also by Jesus, and shall present us with you. 2 Corinthians 4:13–14*

In those days, and at that time, will I cause the Branch of righteousness to grow up unto David; and he shall execute judgment and righteousness in the land. Jeremiah 33:15

Our Father always had a plan to redeem man from sin. At just the right time in history, He put His plan into action. Jesus left heaven and came to earth. He was the plan.

Jesus expressed the faithful nature of God the Father to redeem us as He promised. This same faithful nature is found also in Jesus. His faithfulness to His Father caused Him to die for us. His death on the cross expressed the highest degree of faithfulness. His faithfulness has created our faith in Him. It is this aspect of His character that we can rely on. His character is our faith. He is our faith.

*...and faith **toward** our Lord Jesus Christ. Acts 20:21*

*And, behold, a woman, which was diseased with an issue of blood twelve years, came behind him, and touched the hem of his garment: For she said within herself, If I may but touch his garment, I shall be whole. But Jesus turned him about, and when he saw her, he said, Daughter, be of good comfort; **thy faith hath made thee whole**. And the woman was made whole from that hour. Matthew 9:20–22*

Jesus healed this woman, yet Jesus told the woman her faith made her whole. What was her faith? Her faith was her focus. Her focus was totally on Jesus. This woman knew nothing of faith. She did know that she had to get to Jesus to be healed. Her focus was on Jesus, her healer. Her faith was Jesus, her focal point.

*And, behold, a woman of Canaan came out of the same coasts, and cried unto him, saying, Have mercy on me, O Lord, thou Son of David; my daughter is grievously vexed with a devil. But he answered her not a word. And his disciples came and besought him, saying, Send her away; for she crieth after us. But he answered and said, I am not sent but unto the lost sheep of the house of Israel. Then came she and worshipped him, saying, Lord, help me. But he answered and said, It is not meet to take the children's bread, and to cast it to dogs. And she said, Truth, Lord: yet the dogs eat of the crumbs which fall from their masters' table. Then Jesus answered and said unto her, O woman, **great is thy faith: be it unto thee even as thou wilt**. And her daughter was made whole from that very hour.*
Matthew 15:22–28

The woman from Canaan had no concept of faith either, but she made Jesus her focus. Even when Jesus called her a dog, her focus was steadfast and unshaken. Jesus called this focus on Him, faith. Great focus on Jesus is great faith.

Both of these women showed a great deal of perseverance with Jesus. These women received their desires of Jesus by making Him their focal point. Jesus responds to this type of focus. He demonstrates His faithfulness by responding to our unshakable focus on Him.

Christians get into trouble when we make faith our focus. Our performance then becomes the focal point. This approach of faith is ineffectual. A prevalent teaching is that our faith can change our surroundings and circumstances. Our faith can do nothing. Jesus can do everything. We should focus on Jesus, not faith.

...but faith which worketh by love. Galatians 5:6

Love seems to always be the essential ingredient with God. Faith and love are joined together.

When we love someone, we naturally focus on that person. We are able to properly place our focus on Jesus as we love Him. Our love for God will increase greatly when we meet the Holy Spirit as a person. The tangible love He gives us will energize our focus. When we experience His tangible love, our focus and confidence in God can do nothing but grow. The Holy Spirit reveals to us the loving nature of God. Each time we experience His love, it feels and seems like the first time. Each time we experience His tangible love, our focus becomes directed only to Him. As we experience His expressed love, our love for Him is increased. As our love increases, so does our focus (faith).

It is easy to ask for and expect healing when we feel the anointing or the presence of the Holy Spirit. It is not so easy to expect this when we do not feel Him close by. We can, however, ask, expect and receive His healing when we realize that He loves us. When our mind says He may not heal us, our heart responds with *He will because He loves me.* We depend on His love. It does not change. Our recognition of His love translates into our faith.

For to one is given by the Spirit the word of wisdom;
to another the word of knowledge by the same Spirit;
To another faith by the same Spirit; ... 1 Corinthians 12:8–9

Faith is supernatural and not something we can create by ourselves. Faith comes by the Holy Spirit.

The Holy Spirit is always required for us to place our spiritual eyes on Jesus. Our sinful nature cannot do this. It is focused only on self. It is when we know the Holy Spirit personally and when we spend time with Him that our focus on God will grow. The focus produced by the Holy Spirit is our faith.

Our relationship with the Holy Spirit will teach us that we must trust Him to lead us. If we should need to be healed, He will lead us to the place where we can receive His healing. He may do this by leading us into a desire to focus intently on Jesus. This focus on Jesus may be what enables the healing to come to us. The Holy Spirit may also lead us in a completely different direction yet with the same results of being healed.

We have a very important priority as Christians. We must know the Holy Spirit personally so He is able to lead us to His blessings and protection. As we maintain our relationship with Him, we allow Him to lead us.

Faith relies on Jesus for our right standing with God

GOD'S KINGDOM OF RIGHTEOUSNESS
*for **the kingdom of God is** not eating and drinking,
but **righteousness** and peace and joy in the Holy Spirit.
Romans 14:17 (NKJV)*

*But to him that worketh not, but believeth on him that
justifieth the ungodly, his faith is counted for righteousness.
Romans 4:5*

———∞———

*Faith relies on Jesus for our right standing with God
resulting in a life of peace*

GOD'S KINGDOM OF PEACE
*for **the kingdom of God is** not eating and drinking,
but righteousness and **peace** and joy in the Holy Spirit.
Romans 14:17 (NKJV)*

*Therefore being justified by faith, we have peace with God
through our Lord Jesus Christ: Romans 5:1*

RECEIVING FAITH

He shall glorify me: for he shall receive of mine, and shall shew (make evident) it unto you. All things that the Father hath are mine: therefore said I, that he shall take of mine, and shall shew (make evident) it unto you. John 16:14–15 (Meaning of shew added in parenthesis)

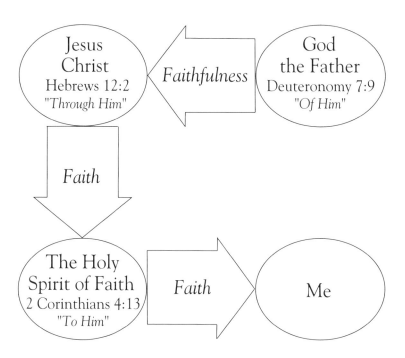

Chapter 8
POWER

*And Jesus came and spake unto them, saying,
All power is given unto me in heaven
and in earth. Matthew 28:18*

GOD THE FATHER

*God hath spoken once; twice have I heard this; that
power belongeth unto God. Psalm 62:11*

GOD THE SON

*But unto them which are called, both Jews and Greeks,
Christ the power of God, and the wisdom of God.
1 Corinthians 1:24*

GOD THE HOLY SPIRIT

*For God hath not given us **the spirit of** fear; but of
power, and of love, and of a sound mind.
2 Timothy 1:7*

The Holy Spirit is often referred to as the power of God. He is not the power. Jesus Christ is the power of God (see preceding page). This pattern is followed throughout the Bible. The attribute of the Holy Spirit's name is Jesus. In this case, it is power. As John 16:14–15 explains the Trinity, the Holy Spirit receives from Jesus and the Holy Spirit makes this evident to us. This is how we receive the power of God. Power comes to us by the Holy Spirit. He is the Spirit of power.

> *But truly I am full of power*
> *by the spirit of the LORD, ... Micah 3:8*

The Holy Spirit is the possessor and the grantor of God's power. This power abides in Him. He desires to convey this power to the children of God. Only this power will defeat the plans and influences of the enemy. However, the Holy Spirit will not impart this power to us if we cannot handle His power. Will we take the credit for what He does or will we give credit to Jesus? It is so easy for us to accept the praise of others. If we take credit and pride develops, we show Him that we cannot handle the power of God.

In years past, I attended a conference of a well known evangelist. During the service, the evangelist called me from the audience to come forward. He had never met me. The evangelist told the audience, "For those who are hungry, this is all it takes." He then waved his hand toward me and I fell to the ground under God's power. The anointing I felt was intense for the rest of the service.

The following night at the service, I felt a tremendous anointing on my hands. For only the second time of my life,

I prayed with the anointing for a woman who needed to be healed. I felt three powerful waves of power flow through me. The third wave caused her to go out in the Spirit. I was ecstatic. I began to believe I had finally arrived. I reasoned to myself that I must finally be at a spiritual level where God could now use me. What a mistake on my part. For the next month, I could not find God no matter how hard I sought Him. I learned a difficult lesson in that experience. I did not arrive. He did. He did the restoration and He really did not need me. God did not allow any pride to develop for my involvement in His activity. It was impossible to be prideful when I could no longer find Him.

O God, thou art terrible out of thy holy places:
the God of Israel is he that giveth strength and power
unto his people. Blessed be God. Psalm 68:35

Power is a subject that yields a variety of skepticism in the church. Many established, well grounded Christians have a fear of power and a disbelief that the power of God is even given to the Christian. This fear and disbelief is not put there by God. Christians are easily deceived to believe that power is not included in our Christian life today. Satan loves nothing more than this particular deception. This deception nullifies what stops him.

Power is indeed given to the Christian when it is needed. God knows every plan and scheme of the enemy. When the time is right for opposing the enemy, the Holy Spirit will impart the power of God to us. He places His power onto our hands. He shows us there is a much needed battle to fight. It is up to us now to use what He has given.

I sometime think of David and Goliath during this time. David fought the giant with what seemed an insignificant weapon, a slingshot, but it was the perfect weapon for destroying Goliath. This is how we can feel. We feel power on our hand, but we cannot see it or understand it. We only know it is real. We enter the spiritual battle with only this weapon. We have the same boldness David had. It does not matter how big the giant is. We are willing to face the enemy and oppose his influences.

The Holy Spirit will teach us that we can send His power to overcome the enemy. As we do, His power will be released from our hand. It is after this release that the influences of the enemy become nullified.

As we develop our relationship with the Holy Spirit, we become accustomed to the power He imparts. The power He provides is part of the protection He provides. If we never pursue the Holy Spirit, we will never know His power. We will experience very little from God until we meet the Holy Spirit. He makes all the difference in our Christian life.

For my thoughts are not your thoughts, neither
are your ways my ways, saith the Lord. Isaiah 55:8

The Holy Spirit will teach us the role we play in praying for others and our role in the ministry of laying on of hands. For our prayers and requests to be successful, they must reflect the same desires that He has. We will not always know what His plans are. During these times, we must learn to step out of His way so He is free to bless as He chooses. We should give Him all the room we can. We accomplish this by removing our desires of God from the situation we are praying over and by directing our attention only to Him. This is the prayer of faith, a prayer focused only on God.

It is very important for us to realize that only the Holy Spirit will impart from Jesus. We must also realize that we cannot impart. This area of submission is where we often fail. During the times when we fail to see Him responding, we can believe that we must help God. However, we must realize that the Holy Spirit does not require our help. Our help only hinders Him. The only help He desires from us is the laying on of our hands. He will often use our hands to impart from Jesus to someone else. Our most successful prayer for others is simply asking God to do whatever He desires for them. Successful laying on of hands occurs when we allow the Holy Spirit to impart as He chooses.

A friend came to my home for a visit. As we were talking, I began feeling the Holy Spirit's anointing on my hands. We stopped talking and began to pray. My prayer was one of welcoming the Holy Spirit to be with us and expressing my love for Him. Our prayers were peaceful and quiet. We held hands during our prayer. The Holy Spirit began to bless my friend. I could feel heat just above my head as we began to pray. I could also feel my hands burning. At one point in our prayer, my friend looked up and told me that holding my hand was like holding onto a live electrical wire. He could feel the Holy Spirit's presence flowing into him and traveling throughout his body. The Holy Spirit was imparting from Jesus to my friend. It was a wonderful time of being close to the Holy Spirit and receiving the blessings He brings from Jesus.

There are several important points to note in this example. The first is that we are to move when the Holy Spirit moves and not before. When I felt the anointing on my hands, we stopped talking and began to pray. Secondly, neither of us tried to get God to do anything. We focused only on Him. We expressed our love for Him and did not focus on what we wanted from Him. Third, our prayers were peaceful and in a quiet spirit of love. There was nothing wild or loud. I have never known the Holy Spirit to be flamboyant or wild. He is always so peaceful and loving. Fourth, we did not try to help Him do anything. Fifth, it is important to understand the experience was totally of Him, not us or our faith.

Efforts of the flesh are not acceptable to God. We have the disadvantage of being flesh. How then can anything we do ever be acceptable to God? Our efforts become acceptable when the Holy Spirit places His anointing upon our efforts. It is the Holy Spirit that anoints our prayers. Our prayers then become acceptable to God. The same applies for laying on of hands. If we should move before the Holy Spirit anoints us, we can get ahead of God and more than likely nothing will happen. If we will wait on Him and move when He moves, laying on of hands can be successful.

When we do anything for God, we should always ask the Holy Spirit to anoint our efforts. We may not be able to see His activity, but we will certainly reap the results of His involvement. Not only will our efforts be easier, these efforts will be much more successful. Only He can accomplish the desires He has given us. We typically omit the Holy Spirit from so much of our lives. We must change course and include Him in all that we do.

When we know God's power we find hope
and enter His peace

GOD'S KINGDOM OF PEACE
*for **the kingdom of God is** not eating and drinking,*
*but righteousness and **peace** and joy in the Holy Spirit.*
Romans 14:17 (NKJV)

Now may the God of hope fill you with all joy and peace
in believing, that you may abound in hope by the power
of the Holy Spirit. Romans 15:13 (NKJV)

———∞———

When we know God's power we find strength
and enter His joy

GOD'S KINGDOM OF JOY
*for **the kingdom of God is** not eating and drinking,*
*but righteousness and peace and **joy** in the Holy Spirit.*
Romans 14:17 (NKJV)

His glorious power will make you patient and strong
enough to endure anything, and you will be truly happy.
Colossians 1:11 (CEV)

RECEIVING POWER

He shall glorify me: for he shall receive of mine, and shall shew (make evident) it unto you. All things that the Father hath are mine: therefore said I, that he shall take of mine, and shall shew (make evident) it unto you. John 16:14–15 (Meaning of shew added in parenthesis)

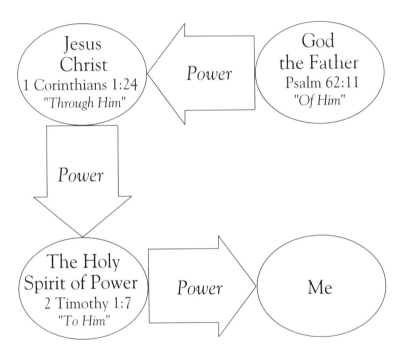

BURNING

---∞---

*And the angel of the L*ORD *appeared unto him*
in a flame of fire out of the midst of a bush:
and he looked, and, behold, the bush burned with fire,
and the bush was not consumed. Exodus 3:2

THE HOLY SPIRIT
And it shall come to pass, that he that is left in Zion,
and he that remaineth in Jerusalem, shall be called holy,
even every one that is written among the living in
Jerusalem: When the Lord shall have washed away the
filth of the daughters of Zion, and shall have purged the
blood of Jerusalem from the midst thereof by the spirit of
*judgment, and by **the spirit of burning**.*
Isaiah 4:3–4

---∞---

…He will baptize you with the Holy Spirit and with fire.
Matthew 3:11 (NIV)

The burning the Holy Spirit brings to us is that of a cleansing or a baptism. It is a cleansing from sin. Evil and sin are purged away. They are consumed. We are also imparted God's holiness. This burning substance of God is His means of cleansing us and causing us to enter His service. After Isaiah was purged of sin, Isaiah volunteered for God's service.

*Then flew one of the seraphims unto me, having a live
coal in his hand, which he had taken with the tongs
from off the altar: And he laid it upon my mouth, and
said, Lo, this hath touched thy lips; and thine iniquity
is taken away, and thy sin purged. Also I heard the
voice of the Lord, saying, Whom shall I send, and who
will go for us? Then said I, Here am I; send me.*
Isaiah 6:6–8

When the Holy Spirit of burning brought the tongues of
fire to the upper room believers, they too were baptized
with the substance of God. They also entered His service.
The fire of God caused all of these believers to intensely
pray. They prayed in many different languages, as the Holy
Spirit desired. These prayers, which were initiated by the
Holy Spirit of burning, caused 3000 souls to be saved only
hours later.

*When the day of Pentecost came, they were all together
in one place. Suddenly a sound like the blowing of a
violent wind came from heaven and filled the whole
house where they were sitting. They saw what seemed to
be tongues of fire that separated and came to rest on
each of them. All of them were filled with the Holy
Spirit and began to speak in other tongues as the Spirit
enabled them. Acts 2:1–4 (NIV)*

*Then they that gladly received his word were baptized:
and the same day there were added unto them about
three thousand souls. Acts 2:41*

And ye said, Behold, the LORD our God hath shewed us
his glory and his greatness, and we have heard his voice
out of the midst of the fire: … Deuteronomy 5:24

The burning spiritual substance of God is given by the Holy Spirit of burning. When the Holy Spirit gives His spiritual substance to man, we often refer to it as the anointing. Many times, I have felt this burning anointing. I have only experienced this on my hands. As intense as this burning can be, once we experience this, we will hunger for this anointing. It is of God and His substance is priceless.

The burning anointing is often more than purging of sin and preparation for service. Many times, this anointing is the substance for spiritual war. This anointing is for fighting spiritual battles.

Our spiritual battle is fought with our words and with the power He has given to us. Surprisingly, our words now carry the anointing of God. God honors our words when the anointing of the Holy Spirit is upon us. Our words oppose the enemy. Our faith becomes tremendously present. There is an absence of fear. We know we win before we ever begin confronting the enemy. He would be foolish to oppose us now. He loses and both of us know it. He cannot match the power of the burning anointing.

When we oppose the enemy with this anointing, we find that we can send this spiritual power to disarm the enemy and destroy his purposes. One second our hand will be burning with the fire of God and the next second it will be totally gone. When the release comes, we know we can stop opposing the enemy. When the release comes, we recognize the need for the spiritual battle.

The Holy Spirit will also teach us how to recognize whether this anointing is for our protection or for someone else. When it is for someone else, He will lead us to oppose the enemy only for the person He desires. The power He has imparted will not be released until we intercede for this person. He will also teach us how His anointing is released. I have many times attempted to release this power and have learned that I cannot release it. My role is to oppose the enemy and only God will release His power. We should always ask God to release His power as we send it to destroy the plans and purposes of the enemy.

God is always gracious to give us everything we need. When He imparts His anointing, He expects us to use it. It becomes a serious matter to be given this anointing only to do nothing. His anointing can then become wasted. The fire of God is too precious not to use. It is given for nullifying the enemy's plans. He has taught me that to not use His anointing is to feel the opposition of the enemy later. But the opposition can be stopped before it ever occurs if I will oppose the enemy with the power He has imparted. I have even tested this. In an attempt to understand the anointing, I have purposely done nothing when given this anointing. In each case, a time of spiritual resistance would be forthcoming. But, if I oppose the enemy when given God's anointing, there is no spiritual resistance. I have seen this repeatedly.

All of this may sound extreme, but it is not. As we develop a closer walk with the Holy Spirit, spiritual things lose the fear that our enemy has attempted to frighten us with. This anointing is not at all frightening. It is exactly the opposite. There is a tremendous amount of strength and peace imparted. We are not alone. We have the Holy Spirit beside us. The understanding is always present that this anointing is needed either for our protection or for the protection of someone else. His anointing is a very natural expression of provision and protection by the person we love.

Chapter 9
LOVE

That I may cause those that love me to inherit substance; and I will fill their treasures.
Proverbs 8:21

GOD THE FATHER

*Beloved, let us love one another: for love is of God; and every one that loveth is born of God, and knoweth God. He that loveth not knoweth not God; for **God is love**.*
1 John 4:7–8

GOD THE SON

*For I am persuaded, that neither death, nor life, nor angels, nor principalities, nor powers, nor things present, nor things to come, Nor height, nor depth, nor any other creature, shall be able to separate us from **the love of God, which is in Christ Jesus our Lord**.*
Romans 8:38–39

GOD THE HOLY SPIRIT

*For God hath not given us **the spirit** of fear; but of power, and **of love**, and of a sound mind.*
2 Timothy 1:7

Love has only one objective—someone else. It is the ultimate blow to self. Pain, hardship and uncertainty—all is willingly embraced where there is love. Only love is powerful enough to defeat the selfish nature we are born with. Love accomplishes a voluntary death to self.

Love is also not rational to our selfish nature. Love surpasses it. Love is patient. Love is kind. Love thinks no evil and sees only good. Love blesses the bearer with an ability to bear all things. Love is willing to endure whatever hardships are necessary for another and the hardships are never an issue. Love does not fail.

Love takes us into a new realm of life. Even the unsaved recognize the value of love. They may not understand what happens to them, but their self nature dies as they care for another. And what a relief for them to be delivered from this nature. The hardships caused by love are embraced and not resisted. Such a high value is placed on another person that they occupy our focus. Only they matter. Only they hold value. Giving to them becomes an aspiration, whatever can be given. Giving the best and wanting the best and praying and asking for the best to be given to someone else. It is God's way for us to live.

Occasionally, the Christian will find this type of love for another. We learn about God as we do. We learn firsthand what His nature is. We understand better who He is and we become more like Him.

God's person is described by love. It is His perspective, one of giving, one of volunteering for death in the place of another, willing and happy to die. The concept of cost was never within Him. His focus was always on us.

God's love is different from our love. His love is without limit. His love does not waver. One scripture that best describes God's love is found in Ephesians 3:19.

And to know the love of Christ, which passeth knowledge, that ye might be filled with all the fulness of God.

We really cannot comprehend a Father's selfless love that would plan the death of His only Son for the person who would carelessly put His Son to death. We cannot understand a Son's selfless love for His Father who would volunteer for His Father to plan His death and then willingly die the worst possible death. We cannot fathom the Holy Spirit volunteering to leave heaven for thousands of years to minister the love of God to people who curse His name and want no part of Him. The love of God is truly beyond our grasp and comprehension. This limitless love is what He yearns to give each of us. His love, more than anything else, shows how far beyond us He is. His love will humble us.

How much more must God do to convince us of His love? He created us to give to us. He gave each of us His breath of life. He gave us Jesus to take our place in judgment. He gives us His Holy Spirit to connect us to Jesus, who is everything we desire. He always desires to bless us. He desires to bless us as much as our heart is hungry for Him. He desires to bless us as much as there is capacity to receive. He desires to bless all needing to be blessed.

*And hope does not disappoint us, because God has
poured out his love into our hearts by the Holy Spirit,
whom he has given us. Romans 5:5 (NIV)*

It is sad to say, but our love for God is dependent on His
love for us. We would all like to take credit for the love we
feel for Him, but we should not. The love we have for Him
is from Him. It is a shocking revelation to learn this about
ourselves. John 16:14–15 explains how this happens. The
Holy Spirit of love receives the love of God found in Jesus
and places His love into our heart. When He makes His
love evident, we respond to Him with the love He has
placed there. The Holy Spirit shows us just how dependent
we are on Him. We cannot even take credit for what we
have within us.

But the fruit of the Spirit is love, ... Galatians 5:22

We will experience God's love when we are with His Holy
Spirit, the Spirit of love. His touch is one of the most
fulfilling expressions of love that we will experience. The
Holy Spirit is always willing to touch us. This is only one of
His ways of expressing His love. Any time we are with Him,
we will recognize the presence of His love. His love and His
touch become more valuable than anything else in life.

As our relationship grows with the Holy Spirit, He will
sometimes remain so incredibly close that for days we will
be stunned by His love. Our relationship becomes so
rewarding and fulfilling when He gives His tangible love to
us and we are able to give back rivers of love to Him. The
relationship is founded in love. The Holy Spirit will interact
where He is loved and esteemed as the person of God the

Holy Spirit. To desire God's love is to desire the Holy Spirit, the Spirit of love.

> *...If we love one another, God dwelleth in us, and his love is perfected in us. 1 John 4:12*

God has called each of us to show His love to others. He enables us to do this by spending time with us. As we spend quality time with the Holy Spirit, self becomes less important. We find someone who satisfies us much more than our selfish nature does. We find His love and find ourselves with the ability to give back love to Him. Now love for others becomes easier. We love others because we love God and we love Him because He first loved us.

> *...for God loveth a cheerful giver. 2 Corinthians 9:7*

Another reflection of real love for God is in our giving. We should give to God only because we love Him. So many today connect giving to receiving. The Holy Spirit teaches us that any attempt to obligate God to give is never permitted. He teaches us that when we give in love to Him, He responds in love and gives to us. This is the only way God gives. He gives everything in love.

A catchy phrase we have all heard in church is *you can't out give God*. This approach of giving to God is unfortunate. Receiving is taught to be an acceptable incentive for giving. If this is the reason we give, we should be reconciled to waiting for an extended time to receive back from God. When we give to God in order to obtain from Him, we are actually attempting to manipulate God. The strings we attach to our giving are the same strings that tie His hands to give back to us. Our incentive for giving should never be receiving. Love is not found in this type of giving. Self is. We must discard the prominent teaching of *giving to get* from God. When we are concerned with what God wants, our giving and love will be focused on Him. He then responds to our love and lovingly gives back to us. God responds when our giving is in love.

And thou shalt love the Lord thy God with all thine heart, and with all thy soul, and with all thy might. Deuteronomy 6:5

It is very easy to say we love God. Only He knows how much we really do. One way we can measure our love for Him is to take note of our actions. How often do we take credit for what God does?

Has this ever happened to you? A friend needs prayer. You pray with your friend and God answers the prayer. Would you feel you deserve partial credit for what God does? Or you pray for someone who needs healing. The anointing is present and the person receives. Would you feel your level of spirituality should receive partial credit for what God does? The answer reflects our measure of love for God. If we love Him as we should, we will never take credit away from Him. He should receive credit for all that He does. He deserves it. We do not. Our level of unselfishness with God reflects our love for Him.

One way we can take credit away from God is if we claim our faith has accomplished our desires of Him. This outlook reflects self righteousness and a lack of love for God. When we know the Holy Spirit as a person and recognize His anointing, we realize who accomplishes everything. Our involvement is minimal. He asks only for our prayers that loose Him to act on behalf of others. If we take credit away from God, He will look for someone else to work through. He will never promote pride. He will promote love.

———∞———

The light in God's love guides us to a life of peace

GOD'S KINGDOM OF PEACE
*for **the kingdom of God is** not eating and drinking, but righteousness and **peace** and joy in the Holy Spirit. Romans 14:17 (NKJV)*

God's love and kindness will shine upon us like the sun that rises in the sky. On us who live in the dark shadow of death this light will shine to guide us into a life of peace. Luke 1:78–79 (CEV)

———∞———

Abiding in God's love is a life of joy

GOD'S KINGDOM OF JOY
*for **the kingdom of God is** not eating and drinking, but righteousness and peace and **joy** in the Holy Spirit. Romans 14:17 (NKJV)*

As the Father hath loved me, so have I loved you: continue ye in my love. If ye keep my commandments, ye shall abide in my love; even as I have kept my Father's commandments, and abide in his love. These things have I spoken unto you, that my joy might remain in you, and that your joy might be full. John 15:9–11

RECEIVING LOVE

He shall glorify me: for he shall receive of mine, and shall shew (make evident) it unto you. All things that the Father hath are mine: therefore said I, that he shall take of mine, and shall shew (make evident) it unto you. John 16:14–15
(Meaning of shew added in parenthesis)

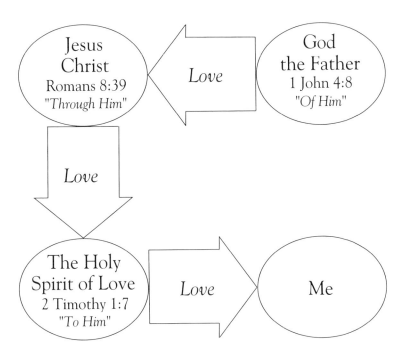

Chapter 10
COUNSEL AND MIGHT

This also cometh forth from the Lord of hosts,
which is wonderful in counsel,
and excellent in working. Isaiah 28:29

GOD THE FATHER

*…the Great, the **Mighty God**, the LORD of hosts, is his name, Great in **counsel**, and **mighty** in work: …*
Jeremiah 32:18–19

GOD THE SON

*For unto us a child is born, unto us a son is given: and the government shall be upon his shoulder: and his name shall be called Wonderful, **Counsellor**, The **mighty God**, The everlasting Father, The Prince of Peace.*
Isaiah 9:6

GOD THE HOLY SPIRIT

*And the spirit of the LORD shall rest upon him, the spirit of wisdom and understanding, **the spirit of counsel and might**, the spirit of knowledge and of the fear of the LORD; Isaiah 11:2*

The Holy Spirit spoke the following to the Apostle Paul:

> *My grace is sufficient for thee: for my strength is made perfect in weakness.*

Paul's response was:

> *Most gladly therefore will I rather glory in my infirmities, that the power of Christ may rest upon me.*
> *2 Corinthians 12:9*

We must be willing to suppress our flesh or sinful nature. We must also voluntarily embrace submission to God in our spiritual nature. Our submission will bring new strength and might. As our sinful nature weakens and our submissive nature grows, the strength of Jesus becomes increasingly evident. The more submissive to God we become, the stronger we are in Him. We must see ourselves as able to do nothing for God apart from Him. We rely on His strength.

> *He giveth power to the faint; and to them that have no might he increaseth strength. Isaiah 40:29*

> *Thou shalt guide me with thy counsel,*
> *and afterward receive me to glory. Psalm 73:24*

Our counselor is Jesus. We are not required to face life alone. He understands firsthand what we are facing in our lives. He will instruct us and guide us through life by His Holy Spirit of counsel and might. He is not limited in how He will counsel us. He often uses His words, the Bible and His anointing to counsel me.

The counsel of Jesus may come to us at the most unlikely times. We will not always be in prayer when He communicates to us. If we will heed His counsel, we will be protected.

My father, brother and I were sitting outside talking when I began feeling the anointing on my hands. I knew the Holy Spirit was telling me something was up, but I did not know what. So, I walked down the street praying and talking to the Holy Spirit. The only words I heard from Him were to pray for the protection of my family. I did.

Approximately an hour later, I walked outside after eating dinner. Immediately, I saw a fire underneath my brother's truck. I quickly ran into the garage, grabbed a blanket and ran to the truck. I threw the blanket onto the fire and the fire went out. After removing the blanket, I could see that the fire came from a homemade bomb, a Molotov cocktail. A coke bottle, filled with gasoline, was lit and placed directly under the truck's fuel tank. The fire had melted a few wires under the truck but thankfully the fuel tank did not explode. The incident was a case of mistaken identity. The bomb was meant for someone else near my brother's home. I was told the person responsible was caught and prosecuted for several of these incidents.

My counselor Jesus communicated to me by His Holy Spirit of counsel that there was something wrong and it was time for me to pray. In prayer, while walking down the street, He instructed me what to pray for—protection. He then answered my prayer to protect all of my family and all of their possessions. He even provided the lack of fear to put the fire out. What a counselor Jesus is!

Jesus, our counselor, desires to teach us, instruct us and protect us. If we heed His counsel, we will be safe. He will protect us. If we refuse His counsel, we will eat the fruit of our own ways.

> *Because I have called, and ye refused; I have stretched out my hand, and no man regarded; But ye have set at nought all my counsel, and would none of my reproof: I also will laugh at your calamity; I will mock when your fear cometh; When your fear cometh as desolation, and your destruction cometh as a whirlwind; when distress and anguish cometh upon you. Then shall they call upon me, but I will not answer; they shall seek me early, but they shall not find me: For that they hated knowledge, and did not choose the fear of the LORD: They would none of my counsel: they despised all my reproof. Therefore shall they eat of the fruit of their own way, and be filled with their own devices. For the turning away of the simple shall slay them, and the prosperity of fools shall destroy them. But whoso hearkeneth unto me shall dwell safely, and shall be quiet from fear of evil. Proverbs 1:24–33*

> *My sheep hear my voice, and I know*
> *them, and they follow me: John 10:27*

Nothing quite compares to the hearing of His voice. His voice is brought to us by the Holy Spirit of counsel. Words cannot convey the importance, the enjoyment, the beauty and the awe of hearing His voice. We are not only hearing words, we are listening to a person. The intimacy of His voice is one of the greatest blessings we will know.

That he would grant you, according to the riches of his glory,
to be strengthened with might by his Spirit in the inner man;
Ephesians 3:16

It is by the Holy Spirit that we are strengthened with might. Only He can touch our inner man with miraculous power. *Might* actually means miraculous power in the Greek word *dunamis*. The miraculous power of His touch cleanses us from the effects of sin.

The Holy Spirit is always willing to touch us. The touch of the Holy Spirit is a literal touch that will be felt. There cannot be a more wonderful feeling than experiencing His personal touch. I mostly feel His touch on the outside of my right thumb while in prayer waiting for Him.

And of the rest of the oil that is in his hand shall the
priest put upon the tip of the right ear of him that is to be
cleansed, and upon the thumb of his right hand, and
upon the great toe of his right foot, upon the blood of the
trespass offering: Leviticus 14:17

The trespass offering of the Old Testament was a holy offering to God that was exercised in the cleansing of leprosy. A male lamb was slain by the priest and offered to God for a trespass offering. The priest would then apply the lamb's blood upon the leper to be cleansed. The blood was applied to the tip of the right ear, the thumb of the right hand, and to the big toe of the right foot. After this, the priest applied oil on top of the blood previously applied to the leper. The priest then made atonement for the leper to be cleansed before the LORD.

Bible commentaries portray leprosy being symbolic of sin. We can recognize the Holy Spirit's contribution in the cleansing of sin as we see the symbolism in this cleansing.

> The lamb was slain first and the blood of the lamb was applied to the leper—the lamb's blood is symbolic of the blood of Jesus, the Lamb of God. This is the blood Jesus shed on the cross. This is the blood of the New Covenant.

> Applying the oil on top of the blood followed—oil is symbolic of the Holy Spirit. This is the Holy Spirit's touch.

> The priest then made atonement for the leper. The result was a cleansing from leprosy. The priest is symbolic of Jesus, our high priest. He restores our inner man from the effects of sin. He restores our soul. He restores our union with Him.

As Christians, the New Covenant blood of Jesus has been applied to each of our lives. Now we need His Oil. We need the Holy Spirit's touch. We need His restoration from the effects of a sinful world. We receive His restoration when He touches us. His touch brings mighty strength and restoration to our inner man. Spiritual waves and rivers flow into us when He touches us. His touch contains contentment, peace, strength and love. Fears leave. The worries of life leave. Any problem now seems insignificant. Our faith in God takes a giant step forward when He touches us. His touch is a very natural expression of His love and His concern for us.

God's guidance and strength keep us in His peace

GOD'S KINGDOM OF PEACE
__for the kingdom of God is__ not eating and drinking,
but righteousness and __peace__ and joy in the Holy Spirit.
Romans 14:17 (NKJV)

...and he shall be a priest upon his throne: and the
counsel of peace shall be between them both.
Zechariah 6:13

The LORD *gives his people strength. The* LORD *blesses*
them with peace. Psalm 29:11 (NLT)

RECEIVING COUNSEL AND MIGHT

*He shall glorify me: for he shall receive of mine, and shall
shew (make evident) it unto you. All things that the Father
hath are mine: therefore said I, that he shall take of mine, and
shall shew (make evident) it unto you. John 16:14–15
(Meaning of shew added in parenthesis)*

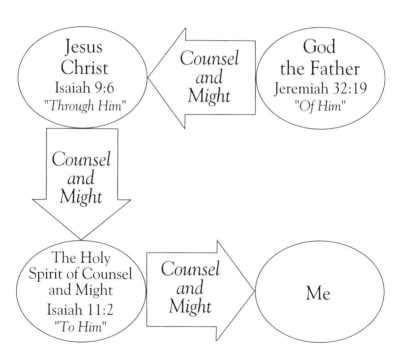

SUPPLICATIONS

In the day when I cried thou answeredst me,
and strengthenedst me with strength in my soul.
Psalm 138:3

THE HOLY SPIRIT
And I will pour upon the house of David, and upon the
*inhabitants of Jerusalem, **the spirit of** grace and of*
***supplications**: and they shall look upon me whom they*
have pierced, and they shall mourn for him, as one
mourneth for his only son, and shall be in bitterness for
him, as one that is in bitterness for his firstborn.
Zechariah 12:10

The Holy Spirit must help us come into the place where we can receive the counsel and might of Jesus. This place is spiritual prayer. The word *supplications* is the Hebrew word *tachanuwn* (*takh-an-oon'*) which means earnest and pleading prayer. In this realm of prayer, the Holy Spirit will give us spiritual ears to hear His counsel. He will also impart spiritual strength into us during this time.

The Holy Spirit of supplications provides the means to enter this realm of prayer. He overpowers our flesh. He removes the hardened flesh that seems to surround our heart. Now we can pray. When He does this, our prayer is deep and fulfilling. Love is exchanged. Deep feelings are exchanged. Meaningful prayer becomes wonderful. He places Spirit within our words. We join Him with our prayer to our Father. The prayer is in Spirit and it is anointed. We pray in a different realm than without Him. We have confidence that our prayer is accepted and faith is always present. His leading causes us to pray the right prayer. Love is present. Peace is present. Our desire for God takes a deeper meaning. Prayer is so easy. Rivers flow into us and flow out to God. Prayer becomes the place we want to stay. Our union with God is now rewarding. His counsel and His gifts become manifested. Our desire for Him becomes a yearning for Him. A longing to give to Him becomes over-whelming because of His giving. We feel we are exper-iencing life for the first time. Everything is fresh. We know He is with us and we are in awe. The flesh is no longer our enemy. It is temporarily suspended. It does not interfere. God is here. The realization arises that we have no adequate way of expressing our affection for Him. We wish we had something significant to give Him, but all we have is our love. It seems so inadequate for what He is giving to us.

This realm of spiritual prayer is where we find Jesus, the strength of our spirit and His words of counsel. We find all the keys to the kingdom here in this realm of prayer. The Holy Spirit of supplications is the only One who can take us there. He leads us into His realm so that He can give to us what He has received from Jesus. He has union with all the counsel and all the might of Jesus Christ.

Chapter 11
GRACE

…for ye are not under the law, but under grace.
Romans 6:14

GOD THE FATHER

*But the **God of all grace**, who hath called us unto his eternal glory by Christ Jesus, after that ye have suffered a while, make you perfect, stablish, strengthen, settle you. 1 Peter 5:10*

GOD THE SON

*And the Word was made flesh, and dwelt among us, (and we beheld his glory, the glory as of the only begotten of the Father,) **full of grace** and truth.*
John 1:14

GOD THE HOLY SPIRIT

*And I will pour upon the house of David, and upon the inhabitants of Jerusalem, the **spirit of grace** and of supplications: and they shall look upon me whom they have pierced, and they shall mourn for him, as one mourneth for his only son, and shall be in bitterness for him, as one that is in bitterness for his firstborn.*
Zechariah 12:10

How can one describe something too good to be true? When John 1:14 says that Jesus is full of grace, He means full. For our unlimited God to be full says something of how much grace Jesus offers. All of His grace is for us.

Grace is being given first prize when we know we should be disqualified. Grace brings a realization of who we are and who God is. When we experience His grace, we realize how lacking we are and how far beyond us He is. His grace is undeserved. This undeserved love and concern is the personality of God. Only by His grace can the ungodly (all of us) be loved. The world being pursued by God is grace. Man deserves wrath, yet grace demands love. Jesus is God's expression of grace. The measure of grace in our life is the same measure of Christ in our life. The Holy Spirit is the provider of grace to God's children. He brings Jesus to us. His grace is found in His love.

Christ is become of no effect unto you, whosoever
of you are justified by the law; ye are fallen from grace.
Galatians 5:4

Jesus fulfilled every rule of the law for any person that will accept Him as Savior and LORD. We no longer have to keep the rules of the law to be acceptable to God. If we believe we can be justified by keeping His law, we fall away from the grace of Him keeping the law for us.

For if ye live after the flesh, ye shall die: but if ye
through the Spirit do mortify the deeds of the body, ye
shall live. Romans 8:13

An important lesson learned is that we will fail in our attempts to keep God's law. We cannot do it. If we truly want to keep God's commandments, we must fellowship with the Holy Spirit of grace. He alone is strong enough to overcome our natural desire to break God's law. If we try to keep the law apart from Him, our flesh is trying to overcome our flesh. The result is futility and failure. Keeping God's commandments is the result of our relationship with the Holy Spirit of grace.

To the praise of the glory of his grace, wherein he
hath made us accepted in the beloved. Ephesians 1:6

The very special Holy Spirit of grace is so wonderful to His children. As we make bad choices in life, our sins alienate us from God. We then ask for His forgiveness. God graciously forgives us. How often we do not forgive ourselves. If we will listen, the enemy will also bombard our mind with condemnation. The Holy Spirit of grace will not allow this to occur for long. We experience forgiveness when we are in the presence or under the anointing of the Holy Spirit. When we feel His wonderful presence, we know we are again restored to fellowship with Him. All our self condemnation melts away. We then understand how loving God is to forgive and accept us. He is so concerned with our well being. The Holy Spirit of grace manifests forgiveness in our life.

The Holy Spirit of grace will also show us our failures and cause us to consider how we hurt Him. It is safe to say that we have not really passed many of the tests He has given us. Our failures bring us to a place of recognizing our inadequacies and yet receiving His blessings in spite of our

performance. He shows us that it is not our goodness, but
His. We know within ourselves that we do not deserve His
blessings, yet He will still give them to us. Failures become a
time when His grace to us will humble us. We cannot
understand this kind of goodness. We know we do not have
what He has. Our relationship with the Holy Spirit
becomes more important to us because of our failures. We
can look back on a circumstance, remembering our actions,
and then remember His. Each time, we recognize He is the
way we would like to be. What a blessing to be accepted in
spite of our performance.

———∞———

Grace provides Jesus for our right standing with God

GOD'S KINGDOM OF RIGHTEOUSNESS
*for **the kingdom of God is** not eating and drinking,
but **righteousness** and peace and joy in the Holy Spirit.
Romans 14:17 (NKJV)*

*That as sin hath reigned unto death, even so might grace
reign through righteousness unto eternal life by Jesus
Christ our Lord. Romans 5:21*

RECEIVING GRACE

He shall glorify me: for he shall receive of mine, and shall shew (make evident) it unto you. All things that the Father hath are mine: therefore said I, that he shall take of mine, and shall shew (make evident) it unto you. John 16:14–15 (Meaning of shew added in parenthesis)

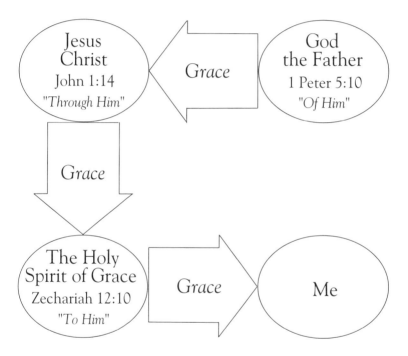

ADOPTION

*To redeem them that were under the law,
that we might receive the adoption of sons. Galatians 4:5*

THE HOLY SPIRIT

*For as many as are led by the Spirit of God, they are the
sons of God. For ye have not received the spirit of
bondage again to fear; but ye have received **the Spirit of
adoption**, whereby we cry, Abba, Father.
Romans 8:14–15*

The ultimate act of grace for the believer is when we are
adopted by God. The Holy Spirit of adoption provides this
for us. He replaces the requirement of keeping God's law.
The law is exchanged for the Holy Spirit. And a new union
is born, a union with God that was not present before. A
union that we will not doubt is in place. The Holy Spirit
makes His union with us known. It is a person who comes
to live in us and with us. Jesus sent Him to us. He came
here to provide our adoption and He leads us to follow
Him. As we say yes, we become the children of God.

*Jesus answered, Verily, verily, I say unto thee,
Except a man be born of water and of the Spirit,
he cannot enter into the kingdom of God. John 3:5*

Our adoption is a new birth for us. We are born of the
Spirit by the Holy Spirit of adoption. We soon discover new
desires created within us by the Holy Spirit. Spiritual desires
now have a much higher priority than before. These

spiritual desires are found within our hungry spirit. Our spirit is now ready for spiritual food. When we meet the Holy Spirit, we will be fed and grow spiritually.

> *And will be a Father unto you, and ye shall be*
> *my sons and daughters, saith the Lord Almighty.*
> 2 Corinthians 6:18

The Holy Spirit brings us a Father who loves us as sons and daughters. Before Jesus, the curse of the law separated man from the Father. The curse of the law being that no one can keep the law. The harder we try, the more we fail. As we strive to keep the law, we fall from grace.

Jesus redeemed us from the curse of the law. None of the rules of the law apply to His adopted children. The rules of the law have been fulfilled for the believer. Jesus took every rule of the law to the cross.

> *For as many as are led by the Spirit of God,*
> *they are the sons of God. Romans 8:14*

Jesus decided before we were born who would become His children. His children will be led by His Holy Spirit. How much more difficult it is for the Holy Spirit to lead us if we do not know Him personally. He has been with us for all our lives, yet He is generally neglected and forgotten. He is waiting on us. When we talk to Him, worship Him, esteem and reverence Him as God, the person of the Holy Spirit, He will reveal that He is with us and He will lead us.

*To the praise of the glory of his grace, wherein he
hath made us accepted in the beloved. Ephesians 1:6*

Adoption also brings God's acceptance. This is such a tremendous blessing. The Holy Spirit will continually show the child of God how accepted he is. In the most unlikely circumstances and situations, we will be shown acceptance. When we know we do not deserve His acceptance, we will still be shown acceptance. This first act of grace provides blessings that we never deserve.

The self righteous person has no need of adoption. The Pharisees of the New Testament were this way. They believed their righteousness had attained an acceptable position with God. Their self righteousness did not require a Savior. Only the unrighteous desire a Savior. The sinner realizes how lacking he is. He realizes what acceptance means. Acceptance through adoption means more than anything.

*…have a commandment to take tithes of the people
according to the law, … Hebrews 7:5*

The tithe is a very touchy subject in the church today. It is explosive because of one remarkable fact. A requirement to tithe is founded in the law.

*Blotting out the handwriting of ordinances that was
against us, which was contrary to us, and took it out of
the way, nailing it to his cross; Colossians 2:14*

Jesus ended the Old Testament law of tithing as a means to find acceptance with God. He nailed this requirement and every requirement of the law to His cross. Now we are free from this mandate. No longer does the amount of our giving affect our acceptance with God. Acceptance comes with adoption.

What a burden Christians can experience if they remain under this law. The guilt of failing to tithe has kept many Christians from experiencing God's love. Galatians 3:10 says those who desire to stay under this law leave the liberty accomplished by Jesus and now fall under a curse. When we trade freedom for the law, we fall from grace.

> *All who rely on observing the law are under a curse, for it is written: "Cursed is everyone who does not continue to do everything written in the Book of the Law."*
> *Galatians 3:10 (NIV)*

It is shamefully wrong to keep Christians under the curse of the law. All of us need to see how accepted Jesus made us. A requirement for tithing to add to this acceptance distorts this recognition. A wedge is driven between God and man when the rules of the law are imposed.

The subject of tithing is still taught in the church today. The fact of this requirement being part of the law is generally omitted. All the other requirements of the law are commonly done away with, but not always this one. But the damage caused by a *requirement* to tithe can be tremendous. The greatest harm is the untrue picture of God that is created. Instead of seeing our God of grace and adoption, He can be seen as the God who holds to rules and regulations. An *imposed requirement* to tithe produces a distorted view of God.

Another somber picture can be created in the eyes of the unbeliever. The unbeliever may feel the churches are only wanting their money. This can keep many from attending church. Is money worth this price? I have listened to several unbelievers express this observation. Sadly, the unbelievers are correct. These do not desire to be yoked to more laws. Many Christians do. For some Christians, tithing can be a means for justification with God—they have kept His requirement of giving ten percent. The one's who do not or cannot tithe can be seen by these as inferior Christians who steal from God. Tithing, like every other requirement of the law, can easily spawn self righteousness.

I remember the change in me when I tithed for the first time. The money I gave was given in a spirit of love as the Holy Spirit led me. My motive was right, but then I allowed myself to come under the law of tithing. I felt that God now owed me something. My attitude and approach toward Him changed as my self nature became evident. I had fulfilled my requirement to God and felt that God must now give back to me. Our love relationship deteriorated. It became replaced with my self righteousness before Him. I wanted what I felt He owed me. The experience taught me about the law and what it brings. The law brought a death to my relationship with God.

It is a wonderful submission to tithe as the Holy Spirit leads us, tithing ten percent or more, but it is wrong when in place of the Holy Spirit the rules of the law are imposed as a means for gaining acceptance with God. It is our heart that matters to God in our giving. Giving is one of our greatest weapons against the enemy and God's plan for giving is founded in love, not rules. We simply follow Him.

I pray that every believer will consider the acceptance provided by Jesus and not allow themselves to be placed under the rules of the law to tithe. It is no longer what God requires of us. He accepts His children because of the fulfillment of His law. His acceptance is His grace. We nullify His grace when we choose instead His law. It is not what He wants for us. He desires instead, our love. He desires a response from us in our giving. It must be love that causes us to tithe. This is our God of grace and adoption.

Stand fast therefore in the liberty wherewith
Christ hath made us free, and be not entangled
again with the yoke of bondage. Galatians 5:1

Before the cross, man was required to keep God's law. After the cross, we are required to accept the fulfillment of God's law. Jesus set the captives free from the law.

Remarriage is a subject the church is required to deal with in the lives of many church members. The question arises, "Can the Christian remarry after a divorce?" The answer is found in our adoption. The Christian is no longer subject to God's law. The Christian is free to remarry because of union with the One who fulfilled His law. If Jesus has been accepted as Savior and LORD, the Christian is allowed to remarry without sinning. Our adoption permits this. Only Jesus can fulfill His law and if His sacrifice on our behalf is accepted, the law has been fulfilled in the life of that Christian. The Christian is free to remarry after a divorce.

Many in the church have trouble with this, but this is the teaching of the Bible. The Christian is free. The person who is truly a Christian will find the law to be fulfilled in his life.

Our failures to keep God's law are now covered by God's grace. This is the new system accomplished by Jesus on the cross, the New Covenant. The striving to keep His law is now our response of love to the One who has made us white as snow in spite of our failures. This is what makes Christianity unique. We do not live under rules to make us righteous. The Christian possesses union with the One who is their righteousness.

> *In his days Judah shall be saved, and Israel shall dwell safely: and this is his name whereby he shall be called,*
> *THE LORD OUR RIGHTEOUSNESS.*
> *Jeremiah 23:6*
>
> *(...the gift of righteousness shall reign in life by one, Jesus Christ.) Romans 5:17*

Many fear that if the freedom we have is known, it will give the Christian a license to sin. Nothing could be farther from the truth. Our freedom causes us to love and adore God. We realize our shortcomings and failures, but we also realize who has washed us clean. He does not condemn those who are not under the law. There is no longer a basis for condemnation. The requirements of the law have been removed (taken out of the way). Thank God for Jesus! He nailed every requirement of the law to His cross.

> *Blotting out the handwriting of ordinances that was against us, which was contrary to us, and took it out of the way, nailing it to his cross; Colossians 2:14*

Chapter 12
KNOWLEDGE

The heart of the prudent getteth knowledge;
and the ear of the wise seeketh knowledge.
Proverbs 18:15

GOD THE FATHER

*...for the LORD is **a God of knowledge**, and by him actions are weighed. 1 Samuel 2:3*

GOD THE SON

*In whom are hid **all the treasures of** wisdom and **knowledge**. Colossians 2:3*

GOD THE HOLY SPIRIT

*And the spirit of the LORD shall rest upon him, the spirit of wisdom and understanding, the spirit of counsel and might, **the spirit of knowledge** and of the fear of the LORD; Isaiah 11:2*

The primary consequence of knowledge is discovering who Jesus is. He is our redeemer from sin and so much more. He has accomplished everything for His children. He is the way to everything wonderful. All He asks is that we accept Him as Savior and voluntarily make Him the LORD of our life. He asks for this so He can bless us. We choose if we want blessings in all things from Him or if we want death and curses with satan. It should be an easy choice, but if we do not have the knowledge of our options, we cannot correctly choose.

It is essential to contain the knowledge of who God is. If we lack this knowledge, we are apt to believe any spirit that presents itself as from God. Knowing the Holy Spirit gives us this wisdom. When we know Him, it becomes apparent what is of God and what is counterfeit. He is the basis for our discernment—how He is, what He is like, how He interacts with us. Unless we know the Holy Spirit, we will have little basis to discern the truth.

Knowing the Holy Spirit makes the discernment of doctrines much easier to distinguish as truth or falsehood. Many doctrines are presented as from God, but many are doctrines of man or doctrines of demons. Knowing the Holy Spirit gives us our basis for truthfully making these judgments and provides a knowing of what meshes with Him and what does not.

Knowing Him also makes it easy to recognize when the Holy Spirit is in something and when He is not. Again the basis is Him. When we become sensitive to the Holy Spirit, He will make His presence known when something is presented to us that is from Him. At other times, we can feel His lack. Knowing the Holy Spirit always provides the direction we need.

It makes such a difference when the Holy Spirit teaches us. He is our teacher. The Christian world has its share of theological scholars who know the Bible but may not know the author of the Bible. There is a difference. Seeking knowledge about God will never replace seeking to know the person of God. Knowledge about Him should help us in our quest to know Him.

Our spirit lives within our heart and is hungry for spiritual knowledge. Only the Holy Spirit can impart the spiritual knowledge we desire. The Holy Spirit receives knowledge from Jesus and makes this knowledge evident to us. This is the office of the Holy Spirit of knowledge.

That in every thing ye are enriched by him, in all utterance, and in all knowledge; 1 Corinthians 1:5

Many times, spiritual knowledge is present before spiritual understanding. The first time I was touched by the Holy Spirit provided new knowledge about Him, but not immediate understanding of Him.

I was praying and worshipping God while lying down. I was just about to drift off to sleep. He chose this time to touch me. His touch was as powerful as the electricity in an electrical outlet. Electricity entered me and spread throughout my body. I was stunned. I was not afraid. His spiritual substance held such a feeling of love. I remember saying to myself that I would never be the same. The day He first chose to touch me was also special. He chose my 38th birthday. What a birthday present!

Receiving His first touch caused me to seek for knowledge and understanding about the Holy Spirit. I asked myself why He would choose the point when I was drifting off to sleep to touch me? It seemed like such an inopportune time. After more times like this, I gained spiritual understanding about Him.

We experience God in a different realm than our own. His realm is holy. Our realm can cause harm to His holy nature. A holy God chooses to reveal Himself to us when our flesh is inoperable. I began exercising this knowledge in prayer. If we will surrender to the Holy Spirit, He will reveal Himself to us. At this time, He will also touch us.

...but ye know him; for he dwelleth with you,
and shall be in you. John 14:17

We should ask ourselves what we desire from our Christian life. If we are content with knowledge about God then the Bible is full of information. Many are at peace with this. Others are not. These see knowledge as the key to learning God's ways and understanding what pleases Him. These see knowledge as the means to know Him in a deeper way. Unknown knowledge about God becomes a priceless treasure. Once this knowledge is uncovered, it is the means for drawing closer to Him. He is the incentive. These see the person as their objective. These desire to understand the person they long for. These understand that once we meet Him, knowledge about Him is never enough.

Knowing God multiplies peace in our life

GOD'S KINGDOM OF PEACE
*for **the kingdom of God is** not eating and drinking,
but righteousness and **peace** and joy in the Holy Spirit.
Romans 14:17 (NKJV)*

Grace and peace be multiplied unto you through the knowledge of God, and of Jesus our Lord, 2 Peter 1:2

Knowledge is a key opening the kingdom of God that is actually called a key by Jesus. When we compare the scriptures of Luke 11:52 and Matthew 23:13 we see the key of knowledge is the same key that opens the door to the kingdom of heaven.

*Woe unto you, lawyers! for ye have taken away the **key of knowledge**: ye entered not in yourselves, and them that were entering in ye hindered. Luke 11:52*

But woe unto you, scribes and Pharisees, hypocrites! for ye shut up the kingdom of heaven against men: for ye neither go in yourselves, neither suffer ye them that are entering to go in. Matthew 23:13

RECEIVING KNOWLEDGE

He shall glorify me: for he shall receive of mine, and shall shew (make evident) it unto you. All things that the Father hath are mine: therefore said I, that he shall take of mine, and shall shew (make evident) it unto you. John 16:14–15 (Meaning of shew added in parenthesis)

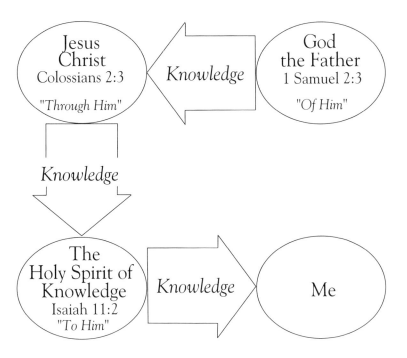

WISDOM AND REVELATION
IN THE KNOWLEDGE OF HIM

*How that by revelation he made known unto me the mystery;
(as I wrote afore in few words, Whereby, when ye read, ye may
understand my knowledge in the mystery of Christ) Which in
other ages was not made known unto the sons of men, as it is
now revealed unto his holy apostles and prophets by the Spirit;
Ephesians 3:3–5*

THE HOLY SPIRIT
*That the God of our Lord Jesus Christ, the Father of glory,
may give unto you **the spirit of wisdom and revelation in
the knowledge of him**: Ephesians 1:17*

All our knowledge of God requires wisdom and revelation
before it will be properly understood and applied. We will
never acquire this apart from the Holy Spirit. He furnishes
wisdom and revelation into knowledge we have already
acquired.

*He that loveth not knoweth not God;
for God is love. 1 John 4:8*

Revelation into the knowledge that God is love will
dictate how we approach God. We should approach Him
only in love. Love will focus on what God wants and not
what we want. So much of our prayer time can be spent in
asking for this and that. How often do we go into prayer
with the sole purpose of loving Him and not asking
anything from Him? A God of love desires true love

expressed to Him. True love for God will want Him, the person, and not something from Him. We actually free God to give to us when we ask only for Him. This gives Him an opportunity to express His love and give back to us. When we ask for Him, we are asking for His Holy Spirit.

God is always concerned with what we desire. We should be concerned with what pleases Him. Our prayers and relationship should be this way. We enter prayer to express love to Him. He always responds with love. This back and forth giving will fulfill all that we desire from God. It should not be a one sided relationship with Him being expected to give only to us. We should allow a giving to Him, giving to us relationship to work. We should show Him that we are most concerned with expressing our love for Him.

Delight thyself also in the Lord; and he shall
give thee the desires of thine heart. Psalm 37:4

The second time the Holy Spirit touched me came several months after the first. One afternoon, I determined that I would pray and seek the Holy Spirit until He touched me, no matter how long it took. I was prepared to stay for many hours in prayer if required, but I sought Him for only ten minutes before He touched me. His touch was half as powerful as His first touch, but still very overpowering. I was just as astonished this time as I was the first time.

The desire for His touch has now become a desire for Him. I no longer seek only His touch. He is the desire of my heart. The revelation in the knowledge that God will give us the desires of our heart is an unshakable truth.

...for he dwelleth with you, and shall be in you. John 14:17

If we look around the room for God, we will not see Him. Is He really there? A revelation of God dwelling with us is necessary to convince us that He is.

I remember the afternoon when He gave me this revelation. It was a sunny day and I was in my den at home. I had been praying. I remember sitting on the sofa and looking up to the Holy Spirit. All I saw was the ceiling. I then began talking to the Holy Spirit. I held out my hand and asked Him to touch me. My eyes were open. I could see everything in the room, but I did not see Him. He then touched me with His unmistakable touch. I felt His Spirit flow into me. I was amazed. I did not see the Holy Spirit, but I know what I felt. His touch enlightened me that God is indeed here dwelling with us. He showed me that seeing Him is not the reality of Him being here. The Holy Spirit not only gave me this revelation, He was the revelation. He is the Holy Spirit of wisdom and revelation in the knowledge of Him.

If ye abide in me, and my words abide in you, ye shall
ask what ye will, and it shall be done unto you. John 15:7

Many Christians lack the understanding of how we receive from God. So much has been promised to us and so little has been received. Revelation is necessary to show us why.

Our union with Jesus by the Holy Spirit qualifies us to receive everything from God. Our union with the Holy Spirit will yield these blessings. So many Christians lack this union. There is a union with the Holy Spirit that is created only by knowing Him. If there is no relationship, this union is not there. The bond of this union is love. A love relationship with the Holy Spirit places us into the same union that all the members of the Trinity have with each other. Our union with the Holy Spirit allows us to abide in God. This new union makes us partakers of the riches of the Trinity. It is now that we can ask what we desire and it shall be done for us. Our union with the Holy Spirit permits us to receive our desires of God.

Chapter 13
JUDGMENT

...he is excellent in power, and in judgment,
and in plenty of justice: he will not afflict.
Job 37:23

GOD THE FATHER

*And therefore will the LORD wait, that he may be gracious unto you, and therefore will he be exalted, that he may have mercy upon you: for the LORD is **a God of judgment**: blessed are all they that wait for him.*
Isaiah 30:18

GOD THE SON

*For the Father judgeth no man, but hath committed **all judgment unto the Son**: John 5:22*

GOD THE HOLY SPIRIT

*And it shall come to pass, that he that is left in Zion, and he that remaineth in Jerusalem, shall be called holy, even every one that is written among the living in Jerusalem: When the Lord shall have washed away the filth of the daughters of Zion, and shall have purged the blood of Jerusalem from the midst thereof by **the spirit of judgment**, and by the spirit of burning. Isaiah 4:3–4*

For all manner of trespass, whether it be for ox, for ass,
for sheep, for raiment or for any manner of lost thing,
which another challengeth to be his, the cause of both parties
shall come before the judges; and whom the judges shall
condemn, he shall pay double unto his neighbor. Exodus 22:9

How thankful we should be for our Father, our God of
judgment. He overturns everything stolen from us. The
above text refers to judges deciding the verdict of a court
case. The Hebrew word for *judges* is *elohiym* (el-o-heem'). It
means God (plural).

If anything has been stolen from us, we have a wonderful
judge to bring our concerns to. We also have a truthful
attorney and a wonderful person to manifest the verdict.
They make up the Hebrew word *elohiym*. They desire us to
bring accusations against our enemy. Satan's thievery can
now be overturned.

...for the accuser of our brethren is cast down,
which accused them before our God day and night.
Revelation 12:10

Satan is now using God's courtroom to accuse us day and
night before God the Father. Satan understands Exodus
22:9. Now it is time for us to accuse satan in God's courtroom. Jesus is our attorney and He will present our case to
our Father. Satan can present his case to the Father if he
chooses. He may choose to forfeit his case and lose by
default. Whomever our Father finds to be guilty must pay
double to the other party.

For there is one God, and one mediator between
God and men, the man Christ Jesus; 1 Timothy 2:5

We must prepare our petition for Jesus, our mediator, to present to our Father. Our first step must be to ask the Holy Spirit to anoint the words we include in our petition.

Our petition must identify what has been stolen from us. This can be anything. It can be a job, a promise of God or anything else. We then accuse satan as the thief. No matter what has been stolen, satan is ultimately guilty. Original sin was caused by satan.

Our petition should include that we have received God's gift of pardon for our sins and that we are now His children. We can ask our Father to apply the blood of Jesus to our petition before we present it. Our petition should also specify a time limit for satan to present his case. This will prevent him from prolonging the case and delaying our restitution. With the help of the Holy Spirit, we can prepare an airtight case for Jesus to present on our behalf. We can trust that our Father will rule in our favor and that we will be avenged speedily.

And shall not God avenge his own elect, which cry day and night unto him, though he bear long with them? I tell you that he will avenge them speedily… Luke 18:7–8

(…the gift of righteousness shall reign in life by one, Jesus Christ.) Romans 5:17

Our Father is a righteous judge. We too are righteous. His gift of righteousness is imparted to each Christian. If we are righteous, we will not lose our court case. We are righteous because of our union with Jesus Christ. Our union with Jesus is provided by the Holy Spirit.

The Holy Spirit plays a significant role in God's judgments. God's judgments of restitution will always be given to Jesus. Everything will pass through Him. He then gives these judgments to the Holy Spirit on the earth. The Holy Spirit of judgment will then make His judgments of restitution evident to us here. How vital it is to know the Holy Spirit. When we neglect the Holy Spirit, we can be neglecting the restitution He has for us.

> *He is the Rock, his work is perfect: for all his ways*
> *are judgment: a God of truth and without iniquity,*
> *just and right is he. Deuteronomy 32:4*

In anything God does, His actions are the result of His judgments. He continually judges us. He knows whether we qualify or not for His many conditional promises. For example, His word promises that if we honor our father and mother, we will be blessed with long life. God has to judge our actions toward our parents. He must truthfully judge whether we qualify for this promised long life or not. There is no point for Him to wait until we are in heaven to do this. He has to judge us now. He is not judging to condemn us. He judges to see if He can bless us according to what His word promises.

> *Honour thy father and mother; (which is the first*
> *commandment with promise;) That it may be well with*
> *thee, and thou mayest live long on the earth.*
> *Ephesians 6:2–3*

God's judgment is His justice for us. Union with Jesus by the Holy Spirit makes the Christian worthy to receive justice in every aspect of life. Everything wrong in our life can be overturned. All we have lost can be restored. All our desires of Him will be met by Him. His judgments show His nature of justice. The child of God will enjoy God's judgments. His judgments reflect His concern and love for His children.

————∞————

God's justice brings joy

GOD'S KINGDOM OF JOY
*for **the kingdom of God is** not eating and drinking,*
*but righteousness and peace and **joy** in the Holy Spirit.*
Romans 14:17 (NKJV)

It is joy to the just to do judgment: but destruction shall
be to the workers of iniquity. Proverbs 21:15

RECEIVING JUDGMENT

He shall glorify me: for he shall receive of mine, and shall shew (make evident) it unto you. All things that the Father hath are mine: therefore said I, that he shall take of mine, and shall shew (make evident) it unto you. John 16:14–15 (Meaning of shew added in parenthesis)

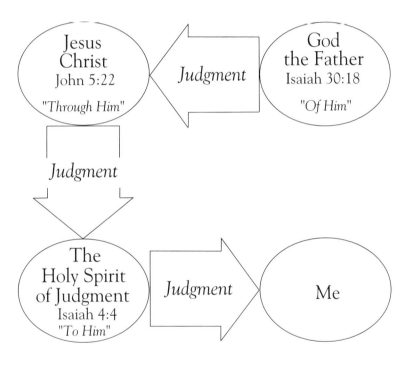

Chapter 14
HOLINESS

Give unto the LORD *the glory due unto his name;*
worship the LORD *in the beauty of holiness.*
Psalm 29:2

GOD THE FATHER

God reigneth over the heathen: God sitteth upon the
*throne of **his holiness**. Psalm 47:8*

GOD THE SON

*… that we might be partakers of **his holiness**.*
Hebrews 12:10

GOD THE HOLY SPIRIT

And declared to be the Son of God with power,
*according to **the spirit of holiness**, by the resurrection*
from the dead: Romans 1:4

I am everywhere—both near and far,
in heaven and on earth. … Jeremiah 23:23–24 (CEV)

An understanding of holiness plays an important role in receiving the Holy Spirit's touch. Before we can find the Holy Spirit, we must learn to embrace the holiness of His person. Holding dear this characteristic of His nature will determine our approach to Him and whether we find Him or not. We must become sensitive to the holiness of the person we seek.

We must also recognize our lack of holiness and the sinful nature we are born with. Recognizing this about ourselves is equally important. Seeing our insufficiency tells us what we must do to permit the Holy Spirit to visit us in the special way we desire.

Finding the Holy Spirit's touch is dependent on our attitude and our approach to Him. We must become still and quiet to find the Holy Spirit's touch. Our mind must become still and quiet. Our mind must have a focus only of waiting for Him. All our thoughts must be quieted. It is a time to be as silent and still as we can be. We must be quietly focused on Him coming to us. As we begin looking for Him to touch us, it is appropriate to extend our hands toward Him and then keep them still. As we begin looking for Him, it is appropriate to express to Him how welcome He is to be with us and then invite Him to be with us. After this time, we begin our wait for Him. We are still and quiet. We are suppressing our sinful nature with stillness and quietness. We are not allowing it to have power over us. We are placing the nature of the Holy Spirit above our own. We are approaching Him on His terms, based on His holiness. We are making it possible for our God to approach us as we temporarily invalidate our sinful nature. This is where we make it possible for the Holy Spirit to visit us—as we nullify our flesh. As we overrule our sinful nature, we remove the hindrance of our flesh to a Holy God who desires to come to us. We make it possible for our Holy God to visit us personally.

In the beginning, it can be difficult to keep our mind still and quiet. But practice makes perfect, and the more we exercise this while waiting for the Holy Spirit, the easier it becomes. The time required for us to wait for His touch also shortens as we exercise our approach to God. What once required thirty minutes of waiting may now take only five minutes to find Him. And before we realize it, our approach to God becomes a lifestyle. Our time of waiting for the Holy Spirit becomes a focus of life that holds great value because it is successful. We truly find God in our approach to Him and find that we cannot live any other way.

It is also easy to believe His touch will not be forth-coming. We are naturally inclined to think this way, but I hope the words written here can be enough for some to hold onto as truth and to not give up on finding the Holy Spirit's touch in a special way unique only to them. *

> But of him are ye in Christ Jesus, who of God is made
> unto us wisdom, and righteousness, and sanctification,
> and redemption: 1 Corinthians 1:30

Holiness is required for us to be acceptable to God. To gain holiness, we must have it imparted from someone who is holy. Only God is holy. Our holiness can only be found in

* *See page 117 for Old Testament reference to the Holy Spirit's touch*

the holiness of Jesus. As John 16:14–15 describes the Trinity, holiness is given by God the Father to Jesus Christ. The Holy Spirit receives holiness from Jesus and makes this evident to us. When holiness is made evident to us, we will have new desires. Sin is found to be our enemy and no longer our friend. Our new desires produce changes that allow holiness to grow in our life.

For I am the LORD your God: ye shall therefore sanctify
yourselves, and ye shall be holy; for I am holy: …
Leviticus 11:44

Holiness is the nature of being set apart as perfect. Christians are set apart from the world by God. Our reluctance to being set apart can hinder this nature from growing. I think of Jesus voluntarily spending His time in the temple as a boy. He was not reluctant to set Himself apart from the world. He was set apart from the other boys His age. Holiness was more important than enjoying the pleasures of the world.

Wherefore come out from among them, and be ye separate,
saith the Lord, and touch not the unclean thing;
and I will receive you, 2 Corinthians 6:17

In the beginning, holiness can cost us. Often friends, activities, music, lifestyle and even our relationship with family must change to fit our new imparted nature. It can seem a high price, but it is always worth the price. We must be willing to place God first in our life and allow His nature to grow in us. This becomes easy when we meet the Holy Spirit personally. He becomes our priority in life. Everything else is secondary. He becomes our focus because we desire Him to this extent. Being set apart from the world is now seen as a worthwhile change. It is voluntary. The world cannot understand this voluntary death to self, but we will and God does. We want Him. Whatever we can do to bring us closer is deliberate and worthwhile. Our longing for God will cause us to leave more and more of our self nature behind. He is more important to us than the world we used to enjoy.

Our willingness to be set apart from the world is what God desires from us, but He will leave this decision to us. We decide whether He is worth our separation with the world. Once we are with Him, He makes it an easy choice. He makes our changes rewarding. Whatever takes us away from Him is seen as empty. Being set apart from the world is the result of meeting and being with God.

Being set apart from the world brings such blessings. The greatest blessing is being closer to God. We will experience more of the life that only He can give us when we allow His nature to grow and our self nature to diminish. It may seem at first to be a high price, but it is actually a blessing. Holiness brings blessings in all things.

For bodily exercise profiteth little: but godliness is profitable unto all things, having promise of the life that now is, and of that which is to come. 1 Timothy 4:8

Godliness or holiness brings blessings in all things. The *all things* should sound familiar. The blessings of Abraham in *all things* are discussed in Life (Chapter 4).

There is an irreversible covenant of blessing that is contained within holiness. We cannot imagine the depth of blessing and substance that embodies this inheritance. Jesus is this inheritance. He is everything we desire. The Holy Spirit of holiness makes this inheritance evident to us here.

... and to give you an inheritance among all them which are sanctified. Acts 20:32

———∞———

A life of holiness is joined to God's righteousness

GOD'S KINGDOM OF RIGHTEOUSNESS
*for **the kingdom of God is** not eating and drinking,*
*but **righteousness** and peace and joy in the Holy Spirit.*
Romans 14:17 (NKJV)

And that ye put on the new man, which after God is created in righteousness and true holiness.
Ephesians 4:24

———∞———

A life of holiness is a life of peace

GOD'S KINGDOM OF PEACE
*for **the kingdom of God is** not eating and drinking,*
*but righteousness and **peace** and joy in the Holy Spirit.*
Romans 14:17 (NKJV)

... that we may live peaceful and quiet lives in all godliness and holiness. 1 Timothy 2:2 (NIV)

RECEIVING HOLINESS

He shall glorify me: for he shall receive of mine, and shall shew (make evident) it unto you. All things that the Father hath are mine: therefore said I, that he shall take of mine, and shall shew (make evident) it unto you. John 16:14–15 (Meaning of shew added in parenthesis)

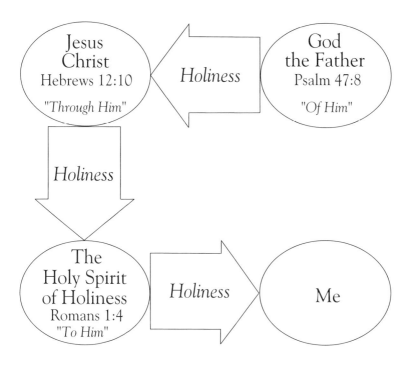

SOUND MIND

And be renewed in the spirit of your mind;
And that ye put on the new man, which after God is created
in righteousness and true holiness. Ephesians 4:23–24

THE HOLY SPIRIT
*For God hath not given us **the spirit** of fear; but of power,*
*and of love, and **of a sound mind**. 2 Timothy 1:7*

The first step of living in true holiness is to have our mind renewed by the Holy Spirit. Only the Holy Spirit can renew us in the spirit of our mind. One touch from Him causes the impurities in our mind to disappear and the true holiness of our new nature to become evident.

There have been times in my life when my mind was bombarded with attacks of the enemy. Ungodly thoughts were present and it did not seem I could remove them. I would seek God, but I did not seem to get very far. But then would come His anointing. His anointing immediately brought a clearness of mind and the attacks were abruptly stopped. Within seconds, my mind was totally refocused. The Holy Spirit had broken the power of the enemy. If I could have refocused my mind during the attacks, I would have. I could not do it. It was by the Holy Spirit that I regained my soundness of mind.

...but this one thing I do, forgetting those things which are behind, and reaching forth unto those things which are before, I press toward the mark for the prize of the high calling of God in Christ Jesus. Let us therefore, as many as be perfect, be thus minded: ... Philippians 3:13–15

One of the targets for attack can be our past. Failures from the past can haunt us and condemn us. The past, when relived in our mind, can easily destroy the soundness of mind intended for us by God.

We all have a long list of failures, but these failures of the past no longer exist. They are the past. Just as yesterday's anointing means nothing today, the failures of the past also mean nothing and should be forgotten. The past should never hold us in bondage. If we have trouble walking away from our past, we must ask the Holy Spirit for His help. He is the Spirit of a sound mind.

For to be carnally minded is death; but to be spiritually minded is life and peace. Romans 8:6

A double minded man is unstable in all his ways. James 1:8

We must choose our agenda in life. We can pursue what we want or what God wants for us. If our pursuit is what our sinful nature desires, we are carnally minded. If our pursuit is what God has for us, we are spiritually minded. The carnal mind brings death. The spiritual mind brings life. A mixture produces double mindedness. A mixture of carnality and spirituality will not work for either agenda. The carnal mind and the spiritual mind oppose each other. This is why everything becomes unstable when this mixture is in place. A definite choice must be made. We must choose life or death.

> *Let this mind be in you, which was also in Christ Jesus: Who, being in the form of God, thought it not robbery to be equal with God: But made himself of no reputation, and took upon him the form of a servant, and was made in the likeness of men: And being found in fashion as a man, he humbled himself, and became obedient unto death, even the death of the cross. Philippians 2:5–8*

Chapter 15
GLORY

Who being the brightness of his glory,
and the express image of his person,
and upholding all things by the word of his power,
when he had by himself purged our sins, sat down
on the right hand of the Majesty on high; Hebrews 1:3

GOD THE FATHER

That the God of our Lord Jesus Christ, **the Father of glory***, may give unto you the spirit of wisdom and revelation in the knowledge of him: Ephesians 1:17*

GOD THE SON

But we speak the wisdom of God in a mystery, even the hidden wisdom, which God ordained before the world unto our glory: Which none of the princes of this world knew: for had they known it, they would not have crucified **the Lord of glory***. 1 Corinthians 2:7–8*

GOD THE HOLY SPIRIT

If ye be reproached for the name of Christ, happy are ye; for **the spirit of glory** *and of God resteth upon you ...*
1 Peter 4:14

The glory of God is His person. God's glory is also comprised of what we may consider as the impersonal. Life, wisdom and understanding, truth, faith, power, love, counsel and might, grace, knowledge, judgment and holiness may not seem to us to make up a person. These do in the realm of the Spirit. God's attributes are His person.

When we walk into a room, our attributes come with us. Our size, shape and appearance constitute our person. When the Holy Spirit walks into a room, He also brings His attributes with Him. His person includes what He brings to earth from Jesus. These attributes comprise God's glory. Each attribute of God's glory is a different name of the Holy Spirit. God's glory does not require size, shape or appearance, yet His glory is His person. The glory of God is His Spirit.

> *Who being the brightness of his glory,*
> *and the express image of his person, ... Hebrews 1:3*

When we read of the riches of God's glory, we are reading about Jesus. He is the expression of God's glory and person. Each expression of God's glory is also an expression of the person of Jesus. The riches of God's glory are the same unsearchable riches of Jesus Christ.

> *...that ye may know what is the hope of his calling, and what the riches of the glory of his inheritance in the saints, Ephesians 1:18*

> *...that I should preach among the Gentiles the unsearchable riches of Christ; Ephesians 3:8*

Jesus really has nothing to give us except Himself. He is everything. He is the glory of God. Our desires of God are all found in this person of Jesus.

Perhaps we desire for God to impart to us wisdom and understanding in some matter we are facing. Asking for Jesus will accomplish our desires. Jesus does not have wisdom or understanding to give us apart from giving of Himself. He is wisdom and understanding. This is where we may need an adjustment in our understanding of who Jesus is.

When we think of wisdom, we naturally find it foreign to consider this to be a person, yet wisdom is Jesus. He is the wisdom of God (1 Corinthians 1:24). If we reflect on understanding, it is also foreign to consider this as a person, yet understanding is Jesus too. He is understanding (Proverbs 8:14). God's glory is expressed as wisdom and understanding. The person of Jesus is the same expression of God's glory.

The following expressions of God's glory are the keys that open the kingdom of God to us here. These expressions of Jesus open the doors to righteousness, peace and joy. Each expression of God's glory will be made evident to us by the Holy Spirit. He is the Spirit of each expression of God's glory.

Life   *...that like as Christ was raised up from the dead by the glory of the Father, even so we also should walk in newness of life. Romans 6:4*

Wisdom

*That the God of our Lord Jesus Christ, the Father of glory, may give unto you the spirit of **wisdom** and revelation in the knowledge of him: the eyes of your understanding being enlightened; that ye may know what is the hope of his calling, and what **the riches of the glory** of his inheritance in the saints,*
Ephesians 1:17–18

Understanding

*That the God of our Lord Jesus Christ, the Father of glory, may give unto you the spirit of wisdom and revelation in the knowledge of him: the eyes of your **understanding** being enlightened; that ye may know what is the hope of his calling, and what **the riches of the glory** of his inheritance in the saints,*
Ephesians 1:17–18

Truth

*… (and we beheld **his glory**, the glory as of the only begotten of a Father,) full of grace and **truth**. John 1:14*

Faith

*That he would grant you, according to **the riches of his glory**, to be strengthened with might by his Spirit in the inner man; That Christ may dwell in your hearts by **faith**; … Ephesians 3:16–17*

Power	*Who shall be punished with everlasting destruction from the presence of the Lord, and from **the glory of his power**;* 2 Thessalonians 1:9
Love	*That he would grant you, according to **the riches of his glory**, to be strengthened with might by his Spirit in the inner man; That Christ may dwell in your hearts by faith; that ye, being rooted and grounded in love, May be able to comprehend with all saints what is the breadth, and length, and depth, and height; And to know **the love of Christ**, which passeth knowledge, that ye might be filled with all the fulness of God. Ephesians 3:16–19*
Counsel	*And ye said, Behold, the* LORD *our God hath shewed us **his glory** and his greatness, and **we have heard his voice** out of the midst of the fire: we have seen this day that God doth talk with man, and he liveth. Deuteronomy 5:24*
Might	*That he would grant you, according to **the riches of his glory**, to be strengthened with **might** by his Spirit in the inner man; Ephesians 3:16*
Grace	*…and we beheld **his glory**, glory as of an only begotten of a father, full of **grace** and truth. John 1:14 (Young's Literal Translation of the Holy Bible)*

Knowledge   *That the God of our Lord Jesus Christ,
the Father of glory, may give unto you the
spirit of wisdom and revelation in the
knowledge of him: The eyes of your
understanding being enlightened; that ye
may know what is the hope of his calling,
and what **the riches of the glory** of his
inheritance in the saints,
Ephesians 1:17–18*

Judgment   *And I will set **my glory** among the
heathen, and all the heathen shall see my
judgment that I have executed, and my
hand that I have laid upon them.
Ezekiel 39:21*

Holiness   *And there I will meet with the children of
Israel, and the tabernacle shall be
sanctified by my glory. Exodus 29:43*

GOD'S KINGDOM OF
RIGHTEOUSNESS, PEACE AND JOY

for **the kingdom of God is** *not eating and drinking,*
but **righteousness and peace and joy** *in the Holy Spirit.*
Romans 14:17 (NKJV)

The glory of God is life, wisdom and understanding, truth, faith, power, love, counsel and might, grace, knowledge, judgment and holiness. Each expression of His glory opens righteousness, peace or joy in our life.

RECEIVING GLORY

He shall glorify me: for he shall receive of mine, and shall shew (make evident) it unto you. All things that the Father hath are mine: therefore said I, that he shall take of mine, and shall shew (make evident) it unto you. John 16:14–15 (Meaning of shew added in parenthesis)

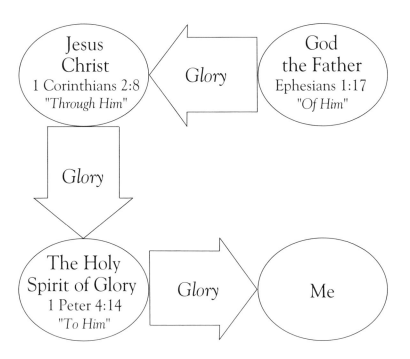

Chapter 16
THE KEYS TO THE KINGDOM

… for the kingdom of God is not eating and drinking,
but righteousness and peace and joy
in the Holy Spirit. Romans 14:17 (NKJV)

The kingdom of God is available to us now. We do not have to wait until we are in heaven to experience this kingdom. The three realms of this kingdom are righteousness, peace and joy. Jesus provides the keys that unlock righteousness, peace and joy in our life. These keys are His attributes of Himself.

It is important to recognize that Jesus does not give these keys to us apart from giving His Holy Spirit. Each attribute of Jesus is a different name of the Holy Spirit. The Holy Spirit will make these keys evident to us. The result of our receiving these keys is entrance into His kingdom.

Romans 14:17 tells us the kingdom of God is found in the Holy Spirit. Jesus Christ is this kingdom. He is everything. All things have been given to Him from God the Father. Each attribute of Jesus that unlocks His kingdom is resident in the Holy Spirit. His righteousness, peace and joy is also resident in the Holy Spirit. Our righteousness, peace and joy are all the person of Jesus Christ. He is the kingdom of God.

RIGHTEOUSNESS

———∞———

...and this is his name whereby he shall be called,
THE LORD OUR RIGHTEOUSNESS. Jeremiah 23:6

Jesus is our source for righteousness. His attributes of holiness, faith and grace unlock the righteousness realm of the kingdom of God. His imparted righteousness opens another door. Righteousness unlocks the blessings of Abraham in all things. These blessings are known as the fruits of righteousness.

Being filled with the fruits of righteousness, which are by
Jesus Christ, unto the glory and praise of God.
Philippians 1:11

The keys to the righteousness realm of the kingdom open our lives to blessings. These blessings are known as the fruits of righteousness and include everything. The Christian has the assurance of receiving these blessings in all things. The Christian has received the righteousness of Jesus.

Love	*The way of the wicked is an abomination unto the* LORD: *but he loveth him that followeth after righteousness.* *Proverbs 15:9*
Deliverance	*Though hand join in hand, the wicked shall not be unpunished: but the seed of the righteous shall be delivered.* *Proverbs 11:21*

Treasure	*In the house of the righteous is much treasure: but in the revenues of the wicked is trouble. Proverbs 15:6*
Family Provision	*I have been young, and now am old; yet have I not seen the righteous forsaken, nor his seed begging bread. Psalm 37:25*
Protection	*For thou, LORD, wilt bless the righteous; with favour wilt thou compass him as with a shield. Psalm 5:12*
Sustenance	*Cast thy burden upon the LORD, and he shall sustain thee: he shall never suffer the righteous to be moved. Psalm 55:22*
Safety	*The name of the LORD is a strong tower: the righteous runneth into it, and is safe. Proverbs 18:10*
Satisfaction	*The righteous eateth to the satisfying of his soul: but the belly of the wicked shall want. Proverbs 13:25*
Wisdom	*He layeth up sound wisdom for the righteous: he is a buckler to them that walk uprightly. Proverbs 2:7*
God's Attention	*For the eyes of the Lord are over the righteous, and his ears are open unto their prayers: but the face of the Lord is against them that do evil. 1 Peter 3:12*

Life and Honor   *He that followeth after righteousness and mercy findeth life, righteousness and honour. Proverbs 21:21*

Remembrance   *Surely he shall not be moved for ever: the righteous shall be in everlasting remembrance. Psalm 112:6*

Prosperity   *He that trusteth in his riches shall fall: but the righteous shall flourish as a branch. Proverbs 11:28*

Happiness   *The righteous shall be glad in the LORD, and shall trust in him; and all the upright in heart shall glory. Psalm 64:10*

Inheritance   *The righteous shall inherit the land, and dwell therein for ever. Psalm 37:29*

Peace   *And the work of righteousness shall be peace; and the effect of righteousness quietness and assurance for ever. Isaiah 32:17*

Establishment   *For the arms of the wicked shall be broken: but the LORD upholdeth the righteous. Psalm 37:17*

Exaltation   *He withdraweth not his eyes from the righteous: but with kings are they on the throne; yea, he doth establish them for ever, and they are exalted. Job 36:7*

Answered prayer | *The fear of the wicked, it shall come upon him: but the desire of the righteous shall be granted. Proverbs 10:24*

Deliverance | *Many are the afflictions of the righteous: but the LORD delivereth him out of them all. Psalm 34:19*

Boldness | *The wicked flee when no man pursueth: but the righteous are bold as a lion. Proverbs 28:1*

Strength | *But the salvation of the righteous is of the LORD: he is their strength in the time of trouble. Psalm 37:39*

PEACE

—∞—

These things I have spoken unto you,
that in me ye might have peace. … John 16:33

Jesus not only wants us to have overflowing blessings, but He also provides the keys that unlock His perfect peace. Turmoil, conflicts and confusion are eliminated. His attributes of wisdom and understanding, truth, faith, power, love, counsel and might, knowledge and holiness provide us with His peace. Each time the Holy Spirit makes any one of these keys evident to us, we enter His peace.

JOY

—∞—

These things have I spoken unto you,
that my joy might remain in you, … John 15:11

Just to make the kingdom of God complete on the earth, Jesus wants us to be tremendously happy. He provides the Holy Spirit with the keys that unlock His joy in our life. The attributes of Jesus that unlock this realm are life, power, love and judgment. Receiving these attributes of Jesus from the Holy Spirit unlock His joy in our life.

> *And he said unto them, Unto you it is given to know the*
> *mystery of the kingdom of God: but unto them that are*
> *without, all these things are done in parables: Mark 4:11*

One evening while praying, I asked the Holy Spirit to permit me to see into the kingdom of God within Him. He gave me a vision where I saw myself standing beside a wall, looking through an open window into the kingdom of God on the other side. As I looked into the kingdom of God, I saw a large cross moving into view. It was right up against the wall. This was not the cross of crucifixion, but instead was a highly polished silver cross with intricate scrollwork engraved upon its face. The ugliness of the crucifixion was replaced with beauty. This was a cross of redemption. The cross was so close to me. It was only the wall that separated me from it. This cross was all to be seen in the expanse of the kingdom of God.

Years later, I dreamed about this cross. In the dream, I learned that we can grab hold of this cross by faith and that our faith can penetrate the wall of unbelief and natural reasoning that separates us from the accomplishments of the cross. I learned that Jesus honors and approves of us holding tight to this cross by faith and that as we do, the accomplishments of the cross are transferred to us. Included in the dream was healing from God.

> For the preaching of the cross is to them that perish foolishness; but unto us which are saved it is the power of God. 1 Corinthians 1:18

It is appropriate to see the redemption cross when looking into the kingdom of God. The cross is where all things were accomplished for God's children. The benefits of the cross are to be received by God's children. Access to these benefits is found in the Holy Spirit. The accomplishments of the cross are found in the kingdom of God within Him.

*Who also hath made us able ministers of the new
testament; not of the letter, but of the spirit: for
the letter killeth, but the spirit giveth life.*
2 Corinthians 3:6

Our New Covenant with God is actually the person of the Holy Spirit. While God the Father and Jesus Christ reside in heaven, the Holy Spirit resides in us and with us here. He bridges heaven with earth. God is no longer far away from us. God is here with us now. The Holy Spirit is the ultimate covenant we could ever hope to have with our Father. Our New Covenant is God living in us and God living with us.

When we receive the New Covenant in adoption, we receive also God's kingdom within Him. He brings the accomplishments of the cross to reside in each of us. With Him living inside us, we find our righteousness established with God. In Him, the New Covenant, we find our peace. In Him, the New Covenant, we find our joy. In Him, the New Covenant, we meet the person of God. Our New Covenant with God is a person. He is the Holy Spirit.

*Now if any man have not the Spirit of Christ, he is none
of his. Romans 8:9*

Chapter 17
OPPOSITE KINGDOMS

… for the kingdom of God is not eating and drinking, but righteousness and peace and joy in the Holy Spirit. Romans 14:17 (NKJV)

But if I am casting out demons by the Spirit of God then the Kingdom of God has arrived among you. Matthew 12:28 (NRSV)	*If Satan casts out Satan, he is divided against himself; how then will his kingdom stand? Matthew 12:26 (NRSV)*
Keys to God's Kingdom (righteousness, peace, joy)	Keys to satan's Kingdom (defilement, anxiety, misery)
Life	Death
Wisdom	Foolishness
Understanding	Confusion
Truth	Lies
Faith	Fear
Power	Incompetence
Love	Lust
Counsel	Deception
Might	Bondage
Grace	Condemnation
Knowledge	Ignorance
Judgment	Injustice
Holiness	Wickedness
Glory	Darkness

And if Satan is casting out Satan, he is fighting against himself.
His own kingdom will not survive... But if I am casting
out demons by the Spirit of God, then the Kingdom of God
has arrived among you. Matthew 12:26 & 28 (NLT)

The Bible speaks of two opposing kingdoms in our world, the kingdom of God and the kingdom of satan. Where do we find ourselves? If we consider the two sets of keys and associate them with our life, we find out where we are. We may realize areas of life lacking the keys to God's kingdom. As these areas become identified, we should always note which name of the Holy Spirit we need. Realizing which keys we need is a first step to overturning these areas of life.

... the ruler of the kingdom of the air, the spirit who is now
at work in those who are disobedient. Ephesians 2:2 (NIV)

Satan has exclusive rule of his own kingdom. It is a kingdom of counterfeit and a kingdom of opposite to the kingdom of God. Each key that opens his kingdom is his replacement for the keys that open God's kingdom. And as wonderful as the kingdom of God is to live in, this kingdom is just as repulsive to experience. Satan is diametrical to God and his opposing nature is reflected in his kingdom.

As we examine the keys that open satan's kingdom, we are examining the personality of our enemy's fallen nature. Death, foolishness, confusion, lies, fear, incompetence, lust, deception, bondage, condemnation, ignorance, injustice, wickedness and darkness constitute his nature. These attributes of his nature cause entrance into his kingdom of defilement, anxiety and misery.

And I will give unto thee the keys
of the kingdom of heaven: … Matthew 16:19

The Kingdom of God	The Kingdom of satan
Righteousness, Peace, Joy	Defilement, Anxiety, Misery

Keys opening Righteousness

    Faith

    Grace

    Holiness

    (Glory)

Keys opening Defilement

    Fear

    Condemnation

    Wickedness

    (Darkness)

Keys opening Peace

    Wisdom

    Understanding

    Truth

    Faith

    Power

    Love

    Counsel

    Might

    Knowledge

    Holiness

    (Glory)

Keys opening Anxiety

    Foolishness

    Confusion

    Lies

    Fear

    Incompetence

    Lust

    Deception

    Bondage

    Ignorance

    Wickedness

    (Darkness)

Keys opening Joy

    Life

    Power

    Love

    Judgment

    (Glory)

Keys opening Misery

    Death

    Incompetence

    Lust

    Injustice

    (Darkness)

For he has rescued us from the one who rules in
the kingdom of darkness, and he has brought us into
the Kingdom of his dear Son. Colossians 1:13 (NLT)

A kingdom of defilement, anxiety and misery, who would want it and what can we do to stay separate from this kingdom? The answer is found in recognizing satan's keys. It is always his keys that determine the entrance into his kingdom.

Have you ever found yourself experiencing intense fear? If so, do you remember the defilement and anxiety that accompanied this key? Fear opened the enemy's kingdom of defilement and anxiety.

Another question to consider is whether we have caused another person to experience fear. If we cause another to experience this key, we can also cause the kingdom of defilement and anxiety to open in that person's life. It is a sobering thought to consider how our actions and words must never cause another to experience this kingdom.

Once we see which of satan's keys holds influence in our life, steps can be taken to separate us from these influences. When we can identify which key we are vulnerable to, we can also determine which key we need from the Holy Spirit. For example, how is intense fear overcome? It is canceled out by the Holy Spirit of faith. Asking our Father for His Holy Spirit of faith will defeat our fear and disconcert the enemy's attempt to drive us into his kingdom. So it is with each of satan's keys. It is by the Holy Spirit that each key is overturned. The Holy Spirit annuls them all. The Holy Spirit is opposed to each key of satan and He is much more powerful than our mutual enemy.

But if I am casting out demons by the Spirit of God,
then the Kingdom of God has arrived among you.
Matthew 12:28 (NRSV)

It is by the Holy Spirit that we are kept far from the kingdom of satan. It is by seeking the Holy Spirit and finding Him that we know Him in each of His names (the keys to the kingdom) and enter His kingdom of righteousness, peace and joy.

Many times an obstacle within ourselves must be removed before we will find the Holy Spirit in a deeper and more personal way. And the more often we find Him, the more difficult this obstacle can sometimes be.

The Holy Spirit's presence is so full of life that this can easily become what we long for. We desire the intimate and enjoyable feelings we experience when we are with Him. However, these feelings should not be what we seek. We must reach the place where we put the desire for those feelings aside. When we can honestly place this aside, then we can begin to genuinely seek the person. Only then, does He actually become our desire, the person does. It is after a time of reaching this place of surrender that the Holy Spirit reveals Himself to us. It is then that He blesses us again with all the feelings of love, awe, sheer joy and contentment that we have set aside. All our desires of Him come flooding into us again. We find what we have always needed and who we have always looked for. It is the very person of God that we find. The recognition of only seeking His person should never be forgotten.

When we find Him, we enter a realm of reality that we believe will never end. We find such life that only He can bestow and the experience with Him lasts. For many days, the reality of God awes us. We feel we have reached a place that we will never leave, but we do. We feel content and we relax. No longer do we seek Him. But after a while, our contentment slowly drains us of Him. His newness wears off with time and we can find ourselves back to feeling distant from Him again. This is where we must be attentive. We must enter the cycle again, the progression of seeking Him and finding Him. Unless we enter this cycle again, we are susceptible to entering a kingdom we do not really desire. A key to remaining separate from the kingdom of our enemy is to be seeking God, seeking His person, seeking Him with all our heart and seeking Him until we find Him.

The Holy Spirit is the Spirit of each key opening the kingdom of God. If we find that our life is lacking in any of His names, it is usually because we are not pursuing our relationship with Him. While He always lives within the Christian and is always with us, how much influence has He been allowed to furnish us? Does our relationship rely on Him as the Spirit of faith to defeat the spirit of fear? Do we know Him as the Spirit of counsel and might or the Spirit of glory or are we content to only know Him from a distance? The latter is the foremost reason the Christian can find life not always experiencing the kingdom of God.

The words of the wise:
Incline your ear and hear my words, and apply your
mind to my teaching; for it will be pleasant if you keep them
within you, if all of them are ready on your lips.
So that your trust may be in the Lord,
I have made them known to you today—yes, to you.
Proverbs 22:17–19 (NRSV)

Instructions for entering the kingdom of God have already been provided by the Holy Spirit of truth. As the inspiration of all written scripture, the Holy Spirit has documented His instructions for us to enter the kingdom of God. He tells us how to find His keys to the kingdom, how to keep them and how to develop them. These are the keys that we must embrace to enter and remain in His kingdom of righteousness, peace and joy.

LIFE

My son, attend to my words; incline thine ear unto my sayings. Let them not depart from thine eyes; keep them in the midst of thine heart. For they are life unto those that find them, and health to all their flesh.
Proverbs 4:20–22 (NRSV)

He that findeth his life shall lose it: and he that loseth his life for my sake shall find it. Matthew 10:39

WISDOM AND UNDERSTANDING

But the wisdom that is from above is first pure, then peaceable, gentle, and easy to be intreated, full of mercy and good fruits, without partiality, and without hypocrisy. James 3:17

For the reverence and fear of God are basic to all wisdom. Knowing God results in every other kind of understanding. Proverbs 9:10 (TLB)

Evil men understand not judgment: but they that seek the LORD understand all things. Proverbs 28:5

TRUTH

Howbeit when he, the Spirit of truth is come, he will guide you into all truth: ... John 16:13

But I will shew thee that which is noted in the scripture of truth: ... Daniel 10:21

If anyone has material possessions and sees his brother in need but has no pity on him, how can the love of God be in him? Dear children, let us not love with words or tongue but with actions and in truth. This then is how we know that we belong to the truth, 1 John 3:17–19 (NIV)

FAITH

... but faith which worketh by love. Galatians 5:6

So then faith cometh by hearing, and hearing by the word of God. Romans 10:17

POWER

But you will receive power when the Holy Spirit has come upon you; … Acts 1:8 (NRSV)

But truly I am full of power by the spirit of the LORD,… Micah 3:8

LOVE

And thou shalt love the LORD thy God with all thine heart, and with all thy soul, and with all thy might. Deuteronomy 6:5

Beloved, let us love one another: for love is of God; and everyone that loveth is born of God, and knoweth God. He that loveth not knoweth not God; for God is love. 1 John 4:7–8

COUNSEL

Thou shalt guide me with thy counsel, and afterward receive me to glory. Psalm 73:24

My sheep hear my voice, and I know them, and they follow me: John 10:27

MIGHT

But they that wait upon the LORD shall renew their strength;
they shall mount up with wings as eagles; they shall run, and
not be weary; and they shall walk, and not faint.
Isaiah 40:31

He giveth power to the faint; and to them that have no might
he increaseth strength. Isaiah 40:29

GRACE

For sin shall not have dominion over you: for ye are not
under the law, but under grace. Romans 6:14

But he gives all the more grace; therefore it says, "God
opposes the proud, but gives grace to the humble." James 4:6

KNOWLEDGE

My child, if you accept my words and treasure up my
commandments within you, making your ear attentive to
wisdom and inclining your heart to understanding; if you
indeed cry out for insight, and raise your voice for
understanding; if you seek it like silver, and search for it as
for hidden treasures then you will understand the fear of the
LORD and find the knowledge of God.
Proverbs 2:1–5 (NRSV)

The fear of the LORD is the beginning of knowledge: but
fools despise wisdom and instruction. Proverbs 1:7

JUDGMENT

"*I the* LORD *search the heart and examine the mind, to reward a man according to his conduct, according to what his deeds deserve.*" Jeremiah 17:10 (NIV)

But I say unto you, That every idle word that men shall speak, they shall give account thereof in the day of judgment. For by thy words thou shalt be justified, and by thy words thou shalt be condemned. Matthew 12:36–37

HOLINESS

But as he which hath called you is holy, so be ye holy in all manner of conversation; Because it is written, Be ye holy; for I am holy. 1 Peter 1:15–16

Who shall ascend into the hill of the LORD*? or who shall stand in his holy place? He that hath clean hands, and a pure heart; who hath not lifted up his soul unto vanity, nor sworn deceitfully. Psalm 24:3–4*

GLORY

For the LORD *God is a sun and shield: the* LORD *will give grace and glory: no good thing will he withhold from them that walk uprightly. Psalm 84:11*

The wise shall inherit glory: but shame shall be the promotion of fools. Proverbs 3:35

Conclusion

We can live our lives in the kingdom of God now. We can also find ourselves visiting the kingdom of our enemy. We know which keys open God's kingdom and which keys open satan's kingdom. Now we must identify where our shortcomings are and do something about them. Realizing what we lack gives us the direction we need. For example, if we are prone to feeling fear and condemnation, we know that faith and grace will defeat these influences. There is now a person we must ask for. We must ask our Father for His Holy Spirit of faith and His Holy Spirit of grace. We will only receive faith and grace from Him. He is here with us to impart the faith and grace we need.

Jesus gave instructions for us to ask for the Holy Spirit. And Jesus said that as we ask for Him, we shall be given Him. Asking for the Holy Spirit of faith and the Holy Spirit of grace is doing precisely what Jesus instructed us to do. We are asking for the Holy Spirit.

> And I say unto you, Ask, and **HE** shall be given you; seek, and ye shall find; knock, and **HE** shall be opened unto you. For every one that asketh receiveth; and he that seeketh findeth; and to him that knocketh **HE** shall be opened. Luke 11:9–10
> (The pronoun it is replaced with HE) *

Jesus also told us that this special prayer will always be answered yes by our Father. We will not have to wonder if this is His will or question whether He will respond.

* See page 35 for exposition of Luke 11:9–10

If ye then, being evil, know how to give good gifts unto your children: how much more shall your heavenly Father give the Holy Spirit to them that ask him? Luke 11:13

———∞———

The prayer of asking for the Holy Spirit will change our life. We gain all that we lack when He is with us. This is how we enter the kingdom of God and leave behind the kingdom of our enemy. We ask for the Holy Spirit and we receive Him. We seek the Holy Spirit and we find Him. We gently knock and His kingdom opens …

Prayer

Dear Heavenly Father,

LORD, I believe you are the Son of God, and that you died on the cross for my sins. I ask you now to forgive me of all my sins in Jesus name.

LORD, you said that you were going to heaven and you would not leave us here alone, but that you will give us the Helper and the Comforter. You gave us your Holy Spirit.

I believe in the truth of God's word and in His salvation. I ask you now in faith to fill my life with your Holy Spirit. Empower me with your Spirit to live the way you want me to live and to do your mighty work that you have planned for my life. I pray for the Holy Spirit to teach me all truth and for us to walk with each other as one.

I ask these things in the name of your Holy Son, Jesus Christ. Amen